# Short Stories

# from our family

# archives

*Spooks, UFO's, Mad people and crazy shit!*

When I was growing up Halloween used to be the night we would sit down with the adults and they would tell 'true' ghost stories of incidents that 'actually happened' to them.

Most families have a collection of ghost stories, the following is a selection of the best of those stories I grew up with, stories which gave me chills and made me hide my head under the covers, check under the bed and listen intently to the night sounds in our house!  It would have been ok but for the fact that our house in those days had its' own ghost or two and the door to the loft stairs was in the corner of my room, I would lie there shivering under the bedspread convinced that darn door would start to creak open very slowly one night!!

Following is a few of those stories, together with a soupçon of the plain daft, seriously stupid and dangerously idiotic.
Remember… when one door opens and another one closes, it's time to move because your house is clearly haunted!

# White Owl Farm

This is the place where I was born in the midwinter of 1962, in the middle of a massive snow storm, the snow lay feet deep, not inches!  My mother went into labour with me during lunch hour, my dad had just finished his cup of tea and was off out back into the sheep sheds to help a few more lambs into the world, but before he was able to step out of the door, mom stopped him in his tracks, telling him he had better 'hang on a bit' as she was having labour pains.  Dad duly did as he was told, after sending word down the road to our neighbour, who quickly contacted the midwife, who in turn was unable to attend unless a tractor was sent to fetch her as the snow drifts were 8 feet deep! Within a very short while I made my appearance into the world, aided very well by my lovely dad, who was completely unfazed and, once the midwife had shown up and checked his 'work' duly went back into the sheds to repeat the process with the sheep!!

It was whilst living at this old farm house in the middle of the woods, that my parents and brothers had a very disturbing series of events, my mother used to relish telling us kids in later years!! I had two older brothers who were not above scaring the living daylights out of my parents in the normal order of things, like burning down the barn, yes, they really did that, and finding the home-made wine and getting roaring drunk, they were 6 and 8 at the time and really did that too! My mother caught sight of the two of them in the field next to the house, they were both tottering around and kept falling over, she ran down to them, thinking there must be something seriously wrong with the pair of them. That is, until she got there and found the empty bottle of Parsnip wine, they were literally falling down drunk! They were made to drink copious amounts of water and my mother made them walk around and around the field until they had sobered up, then she gave them hell!

The daftest one my elder brother Freddy did, (which affected my poor old dad for years to come), was when the boys, who used to love to climb on the flat kitchen roof and run along it like idiots, came up with a great idea! They were running along the kitchen roof when my dad came out of the kitchen door and my older brother shouted from above 'catch dad' and leapt off the roof fully expecting dad to catch, which he duly did, but nearly ripped his shoulders out of socket and suffered with them for the rest of his life!!

Anyway, life went on in this old house, my mom always said it was 'haunted' she said it had an odd atmosphere and although she didn't know the history of the place at the time, was convinced someone had died there. She always used to duck her head when she came out of the main front door, couldn't explain why, but felt compelled to duck. She later found out that someone had hung themselves out of the window that was directly above the front door and their feet hung down in front of the doorway until they were found and cut down, which we were told took a couple of days as he was a single farmer and nobody went there much!!

My dad was working both on the smallholding and, also had a job doing nights elsewhere to make ends meet, resulting in his being away from the farm overnight several nights a week. Mom used to hate these nights, she would regularly gather us three kids together and we would all sleep in the same room, with my mother having a loaded shot gun by the bed, 'just in case', she used to say.

She always felt fearful and defensive in that house! Many nights she would wake up and would think there was someone looming over the end of the bed, she would leap out of bed, and by the time she had lit the candle (no electricity in that house, it was too far away from civilisation!), she would look again and there was never anybody there. She would also feel that someone was watching her when she was cooking in the kitchen, feeling compelled to keep looking round, but there was never anyone there. Things would go missing regularly and turn up in the most unusual places. She would be stirring the stew, put the spoon down, turning to do something quickly, look back and the spoon would be gone, turning up somewhere odd, like the outhouse, or the barn. Used to drive her mad!! Dad of course, didn't believe in any of that nonsense until one day, even he had to admit there was something 'odd' about that old farm house!

I was far too small to have any meaningful input into this story, but I am told I was sleeping peacefully in my day cot in front of the fire through the whole thing! (Some things never change!!).

It was early morning, still not quite light, Dad had just returned from his 'night' work and was just about to head out to the barn to feed the animals before he went to bed. Mom was making some porridge in the kitchen on the old range we had in those days. My brothers were not up yet, although had been shouted at several times for their tardiness!! Suddenly there was a commotion upstairs and the boys came running down the stairs like the hounds of hell were on their tails!! My mother laughed and asked if they had 'wet the bed' as they were in such a rush! Both boys, instead, looked terrified and Dad, noting this, asked what was wrong.

'There's someone upstairs said my older brother, 'yeah' chimed in the smaller of the two, 'there was a man and he was watching us'.

Dad burst into action and hightailed it up the stairs in order to catch the intruder. He ran from room to room, finding nothing, came back downstairs to two terrified children and my mother reaching for the 12-bore shotgun! 'There's nobody up there…. what did you see?' he asked.

The boys both started talking at once, like angry sparrows, fighting in a hedgerow. 'There was a man, he was in our bedroom', they both chirped in unison. Their room being the one at the front of the house, the window of which was the one my mother had such an issue with! My elder brother, being the more steadfast of the two, gave the following description…'he was a scruffy man, was about the same age as Dad, dressed in ragged clothing, he looked angry or sad, either way, he wasn't very happy', 'he made funny growly sound' the younger added. As soon as they heard the growly noise it spurred them into action and they ran downstairs.

My dad, not quite sure what the heck was going on, plodded back upstairs and did a thorough search of the whole floor, looking under beds, in wardrobes, in fact anywhere he figured a man could hide, he came up with nothing, and nobody had come down the stairs as my mom was standing in the kitchen at the bottom of the stairs with a loaded gun!

Dad was due to work again that night and my mother was not at all happy about him going, she barricaded the bedroom door and had both the 12 bore shotguns fully loaded by her side of the bed, with the boys in the other side and me in a cot next to them, she wasn't taking any chances!! The night was quiet and morning took an absolute age to arrive. When my Dad got back in that morning, he had a funny look on his face, didn't stop to say good morning to anyone, but shot up the stairs at a rate of knots. Mom heard him running into the boys' bedroom, stomping about and shouting. 'C'mon you bugger, let's have you'. After a long few minutes, he came back downstairs and plonked himself in the chair by the fire, he looked confused and dumfounded. Mom asked whatever the matter was, and was stumped when he said...'I was coming down the lane, looked up at the front of the house and there was a man looking out of the boys' bedroom window!!' My mother nearly dropped the pan she was holding, she asked if it looked like the man the boys had seen and indeed it did! They discussed this at length and decided that they wouldn't tell anyone else in the village, as nobody would believe them anyway. My mother was still adamant about carrying a loaded shotgun up to bed, even if it was something otherworldly, as far as she was concerned, it would get both barrels if he/it showed up again!

I have some very early memories of that house, and can clearly remember being in my cot and also a pram being wheeled outside a supermarket. One of my clearest early memories is of being in a 'den' in the barn, the boys had made a tunnel right down into the bottom of the straw bales and I clearly remember climbing into it, I also remember them lighting a candle as it was dark in there....

the obvious result was the entire barn becoming a towering inferno.

I have a hazy memory of being pulled by my arms out of those burning bales, my dad must have been the one to pull me out, as my brothers were not very big themselves. I can remember watching the whole thing going up with flames shooting into the sky and the fire brigade turning up. Sometimes, just sometimes, I think back to that day and how close I came to never growing up at all, I was around 3 or 4 at the time.

Another happier memory of that place is of snow, lots and lots of snow, my dad made us a huge sledge out of the top of a car, he used an oxy acetylene torch to cut the roof off the car, welded bars onto the sides and a rope was attached to the front.

He towed that massive sledge up to the top of a small hill opposite the farmhouse, we called it the 'pinnacle'

(pictured)

We all jumped aboard and sped down the hill, through the gate at the bottom of the hill, straight across the road and right up to the back-kitchen door. We did this again and again, my mom and dad were like kids, running us all back up that hill, leaping on the sledge and screaming with laughter as we shot down again and again. There was never any danger of any cars being on that road, there were snow drifts along the whole length of the road, no cars have been down there for days and wouldn't be for days yet to come.

As we approached Christmas time whilst living at that house, before the snow came, we were all in my dad's old Austin, heading home one evening. Us three kids were in the back, mom and dad in the front. As we were heading through a particularly wooded area about 2 miles from the house, a large antlered Stag suddenly appeared on the road in front of us, running for its life. My dad could only see several hundred pounds of venison on the hoof and put his foot down, no doubt thinking of all that lovely grub. Us kids on the other hand, could only think that this must be Santa's Reindeer, we screamed and screamed, mom joined in and dad's shoulders slumped in defeat, he slowed the car and watched all that meat jump over the brook and head off, no doubt to meet up with Rudolf! Dad quickly dropped us off at home, grabbed the 12-bore shotgun and headed out, determined not to be done out of all that venison steak he had been dreaming about. He was gone for hours, but sadly for him, never had a sniff! Us kids were delighted, Santa would not be down one reindeer that year!

There were a few other odd happenings at that old house, nothing as definitive as the man in the bedroom, indeed, he didn't put in any further appearances to my parents' knowledge, indeed, she had moved the boys out of that room quite soon after those events.  As far as my mother was concerned, that was the end of that, my mother was insistent that the whole family be moved immediately, it took a month, but they soon settled in somewhere else!

# Old Tommy

The new place was a lovely cottage in a village not too far from the old house, the cottage was attached to the one next door, where a lovely old man called Tommy lived. He and my parents got on really well, they all had a love of the area and the wonderful gardens that both places had behind them. The gardens were some one hundred feet long and both were stuffed to the gunnels with vegetables, they used to share the bounty when everything came to fruition. Those were remembered by my mother as wonderful years, with us 3 children all under ten and growing fast, full of cheek and energy. We all loved Tommy and he loved us, we would be in his house, just as much as our own and he loved us being there, loved the hustle and bustle and the noise, he had never had a family, my mom always said he would have been a marvellous dad, he treated us kids so well!

He was about 30 years older than my parents and sadly one day my mother went around to take him some Apple

Crumble she had just made and found him dead on the kitchen floor. She was devastated, as were we kids. Dad tried to find out if he had any family, but it seemed, if he did, they couldn't be found, it was all very sad. Dad and mom paid for his funeral, a simple affair, there was a fair contingent of the rest of the village turned out for the funeral and as was tradition in those days, it was everyone, including kids, back to the pub for a proper wake!

A few weeks had passed since Tommy had died and we were all missing him. Life went on, his house had been emptied of all its's furniture and as it belonged to the church, there was no money to speak off, what little there was, Dad used to provide a headstone for Tommy, it was the least he felt he could do.

One Sunday morning, a week or so later, mom went to turn on the tap in the kitchen for some water to boil a kettle, it wouldn't work…'odd' she thought, this only happened when Tommy was alive, the pipes were connected to one another, as was usual in those days, when one household turned on the tap, the other couldn't get any water until the neighbouring household turned theirs off. Mom was perplexed, however, the water suddenly began to flow, so she didn't think any more of it. Dad came in from the garden and mom mentioned the tap to him, he just thought it was 'something and nothing' which was the saying in those days, if you didn't have a freaking clue but didn't want to look stupid!

Dad started to wash his hands, ready for dinner to be served, he turned on the tap, nothing, it was all quiet, the boys and myself were out on the village green playing. Dad listened and was shocked to hear the sound of a tap running next door…! 'What the heck', he ran out of the back door and round to next doors kitchen window which was right next to ours, he could clearly see the sink, which was the old Belfast type, and was shocked to see that it was completely bone dry and there was even a cobweb across the sink which had not been disturbed! He couldn't quite believe his eyes, went back to our kitchen and grabbed the spare key to Tommy's place that we kept by our back door. He went around again, opened the back door next to the kitchen sink and confirmed his original sight…. all was quiet and undisturbed; the sink was bone dry and a spider had even take taken up residence in the sink!!

Dad was utterly surprised by this, he thought he must have been dreaming, went back next door to our house, mom was waiting in the kitchen, no doubt hoping for an explanation, when none was forthcoming, they both decided it must be down to something else, maybe the water main had been switched on and off. Dad asked round the neighbours if they were having trouble with their water supply, but no, none of them had.

My parents had this happen to them again and again, they never could find an explanation. The other thing that happened whilst they were living there, which was also pretty unexplainable, and to mom, who it happened to, quite unnerving. It was again about a month or so after Tommy died, she was at the sink (when did mom's in those days spend their days anywhere else?), when she heard footsteps, hobnail boot footsteps, approaching the window from Tommy's side. There was a cobblestone path under the windows across the back of those houses, and men in those days invariably wore hobnail boots. She was taken aback, and waited to see who it was, as nobody should have been next door, and if anyone was due, they would call in first to my parents who had the keys. She stood there rooted to the spot as the boots stomped past the kitchen window, paused directly in front of her, then marched on before fading away. She was completely freaked out when she looked out of the window and nobody could be seen! She was even more freaked out when she looked at the clock, it was 9.30 in the morning, Tommy always left his house at precisely 9.30 every morning to collect his paper, he always used to pause and wave to mom as he passed the window, seems Tommy was still doing just that!! This happened quite a lot over the coming months, even to the point that my mother became quite comfortable with Old Tommy, the friendly ghost!

# Canwell Hall

*Canwell Hall - 17ᵗʰ Century Manor House in the Midlands.*

During the 1950's, when my mother was training to be a nurse, her and all the other trainees were based at Canwell Hall for the duration of their training, other areas of the house being used as a hospital for sick children shortly after the Second World War.

The nurses were roomed at the top of the house in the old servants' quarters, as if that wasn't spooky enough, they used to wheel the bodies out under their windows in the dead of night!

My mother settled well into nursing, she had some lovely friends and they were all a pretty dedicated bunch, except one that is, who 'did a bunk' in the middle of the night after being asked to do the obligatory 'laying out of a new born infant'. This was something they were all put through at some point or another, (a sort of 'initiation' rite that all trainees got asked to do in the early weeks of training), most just got on with the job in hand, in floods of tears, but managed to finish the grisly task.

One winters' evening, when five of the nurses had finished their shift and were walking back to their dorms, my mother and one of her friends were startled to see a very fine lady strolling across the lawns, in full flowing riding habit. My mother made a comment to the others with her and nobody but that one other nurse could actually see this woman, as the 'chosen' two watched in fascination, said lady glided along and simply faded away before their eyes, they were totally spooked by the whole experience.

A few months into the training, my mother was sharing a bedroom with four other nurses, it was in the eaves at the top of the house and, pretty spooky up there. The nurses were usually on different shifts so arrived back for a sleep at all different times of the day and night. My mother had just returned off a night shift, it was very early in the morning, as she walked through the door, being as quiet as she could, so as not to wake the other occupants, she nearly jumped out of her skin, when the door she had just closed slowly opened and a shadowy figure glided into the room. Awakened by my mother's squeak of alarm one of her roommates also saw the shadowy figure, rather closer than she would have liked. It glided straight through her bed and into a wardrobe on the other side of the room. All pretence at quiet was dropped as said nurse let out a blood curdling screech, my mother joined in, there was only one other occupant of the room that night who had a very rude awakening, she, of course, joined the cacophony, however she did later admit she hadn't seen a thing, just woke up screaming because the others were!

The entire house was in uproar, lights going on everywhere, including the dreaded Matron's, in those days they tended to be a bit of a harridan and this one was no different. She gave my mother and her startled, shaking, roommates a dressing down that had them all quaking in their boots for entirely another reason! When everything had calmed down a few days later, the Matron called my mother and the other nurses who shared that room into a meeting, she told them that a nurse had hung herself in that wardrobe a couple of years before. Then told them 'not to be so bloody stupid as ghosts can't hurt you', and if she heard any more about it, they would be sent home with a flea in their ears!! Needless to say, even though they did see the 'nurse' a couple more times, none of them dared say a word, the Matron was considerably scarier than some stupid ghost!!

My mom used to love regaling us with tales of those wards, some of the children had special needs and could be quite 'naughty' on occasion. One in particular used to lay in wait for any new members of staff who didn't know what to expect. He would collect his 'special surprise' and wait with baited breath for someone unsuspecting to come through the door. He would then leap up in the air, let out a blood curdling scream and throw a large handful of poo, with alarming accuracy, at the poor victim! He invariably hit them square in the face, didn't make a distinction between doctors, nurses or indeed unsuspecting visitors!

The nurses would spend many afternoons trying to calm the ruffled feathers of someone whose face was smeared with poo. They used to be entirely professional until they were out of earshot, when they would all collapse in hysterics, that kid became a firm favourite when he got the Matron with a beautiful shot one afternoon!

# The 'UFO'

Although not strictly a ghost story, this is a story that both my parents loved to re-tell again and again over the years, it affected them so profoundly!

One of my brothers was 6 weeks old at the time, so I can pinpoint the date to around mid-October of 1958. The place was a small village called Comberford, not far from Lichfield. As it was a clear early evening and had been one of those beautiful Autumn days we all dream about, my parents decided, as it was such a lovely day, to take a walk to the local pub. It was about a mile and a half up the lane, they set off with the baby in the pram and my 2-year-old brother sat on top of the pram in one of those chair attachments they used in those days. They stayed for a drink or two and sat in the garden outside the pub with the kids. Afterwards, on walking back down the lane, they decided to stop in a gateway and both of them were 'star spotting', with my dad pointing out the constellations to my mother. They had spotted the Great Bear, Orion etc, when my mother looked again and was surprised to see a portion of the sky completely black with no stars at all, she pointed this out to my dad and they were both trying to work out what it was as there were no clouds in the sky whatsoever.

After standing in the gateway, dad leaning on the gate, they watched this 'black patch' for a few minutes and were startled to see it suddenly become illuminated. It was a massive 'wheel of light' and the lights were going around and around the 'wheel' shape. As they both stood there transfixed, a number of smaller 'lights' were seen to come out of the main 'wheel' and fluttered about the sky. My dad, being the much braver of the two (or most stupid??), thought it would be a good idea to take his torch out and start flashing his light at the 'ship' in the sky. My mother nearly wet herself with fear when he did this, she grabbed the pram and started hightailing it down the lane back towards the house. My dad gave it a final flash – at which point all the smaller points of light shot back into the main 'ship' and it suddenly sped off into the distance at such a speed my dad had trouble keeping up with it with his eyes. My mother had stopped when he shouted and was just in time to catch it speeding off into the distance. They talked about it all the way home and until late into the evening, they eventually concluded that nobody would believe them anyway, so decided not to tell anyone. Indeed, they kept this pact right up until one night when I was about 10, (I hadn't been born at the time of these events!), they both came out with this amazing story, they were quite shy about it at first, but then got quite animated and were finishing each other's sentences, confirming the series of events etc., they had us kids spellbound with the story!

***

It wasn't until around 1999 that I had a similar sighting, I was with my dad at the time, my mother had died in 1995. We were stood outside in the back yard of our house, in total darkness, would be about November time, again looking at the night sky, checking out the constellations, when, out of the corner of my eye, I could see something moving, I mentioned it to dad and we were both spellbound by the sight of a 'classic' triangular craft with a light in each point, flying low and totally silent over our heads. It was massive! We couldn't believe our eyes, we are on the flight path to Bristol airport so know what planes look and sound like, and this wasn't any type of plane we had ever seen!! I have not told too many people, the usual reason, the ridicule!! It wasn't a V2 (Vulcan Bomber), which is the usual 'go to' for the common or garden sceptic, how do I know? I have seen the V2 several times flying low and slow at the air show here where I live, if it had been a V2, it would have rattled the windows out of their frames and the teeth from our heads! The noise would have had everyone out on the street, when in fact what we saw was totally silent! It glided slowly overhead and disappeared off towards the west. We were both totally gobsmacked!

I think the story that convinced me there is more to this than meets the eye was an encounter that happened on West Quantoxshead in the 80's. A man in his 60's was walking his dog on the moorland around this area of the Quantocks, he was startled to see an almost black/dark grey, extremely shiny triangular craft in the distance, he thought it must be a new type of military jet, until it rushed up to just above his head and stopped dead. He said it was the size of 2 double decker buses side by side, so quite large. He was so frightened he just stood there and didn't move a muscle. It suddenly flew off, totally silently, and at massive speed.

He didn't tell anyone, not even his wife, for fear that nobody would believe him. It wasn't until a few days later when he started noticing his face was burning red and so were his hands. His face began to blister and he went to his doctor who could find no cause for it. It was only as this point he made a tentative contact with BUFORA, whom he swore to secrecy, he still hadn't admitted to his wife at this point what had happened. They were able to interview him, anonymously of course, and arrange for him to have treatment for his 'radiation burns' for that's what they were. It was only at this point he told his wife, as he was worried that she might have come into contact with radioactivity in the course of washing his clothes.

To date, this still remains anonymous.  Why would anyone make up something like this?  To include radiation burns??

When you stop to think about it though, what an amazing way to explore another World??  Fly all over it at will, being seen by thousands every night, and yet nobody actually believes you are real, because to that society you are a joke??  Couldn't have made it up, could you??  To the total sceptic, I will say this, UFO's absolutely exist, of that there is no doubt.  It is what they are, and what they represent, now that *is* up for debate!

# Mill House

This is the house I grew up in, it was a classic two up, two down, country cottage with Agar, outside toilet and bats in the loft! When we moved in, the back part of the house was basically a 'lean-to' with a tin roof, there was a brick floor with a gully running down the back of the house, we didn't find out what this gully was for until it rained. It was then we realised we had a house with not only running water, but a running stream, right through the back 'kitchen'. It was weird, people had obviously been living with this odd 'indoor plumbing' for years, they had even thoughtfully fashioned a channel for the water, hilarious!

I had never 'seen' or 'heard' anything there in the early years, it wasn't until my elder brother got killed in a tragic accident at age 16 in 1973, that odd, unexplainable things began to occasionally happen.

The first of which, my mother and her best friend Cynthia were both witness to, it was about 2 months after my brothers' death in 1973, it was late spring so the windows were all open, the sun was shining, it was a classic 'beautiful day'. My mother and her friend were sat in the kitchen of the house, talking quietly about my brother, they were about to clear out all his clothes and had a couple of pairs of his shoes on the floor in the kitchen, trying to decide what they should do with everything. In particular, one pair of boots that he had painted silver, glam rock was massive in those days!! These particular boots being silver was causing some gentle humour between my mother and her friend, they were trying to decide who would possibly wear those boots! As they were laughing at the possibilities, those darn boots lifted about a foot in the air, wiggled about, then fell to the floor again. Needless to say, both ladies were gobsmacked and totally taken aback by this turn of events. My mother told me later that they just sat their staring at those damn boots waiting to see if they would do anything else. They didn't move again, and both my mother and Cynthia were convinced it was my brother, just letting them know he was 'still about'!

As a follow up to this story, about 2 weeks later, after my mother had put those boots in a cupboard as she decided that she couldn't bear to be parted from them after all. When she went back into that cupboard, the boots were missing, she looked everywhere, we were all questioned as to whether anyone had moved them, which nobody had, it was all a bit of a mystery. We never did find them…

Several weeks after these events, and aunt came to visit, she was one of those 'spooky' types who often visited spiritualist churches and mediums, caused us all to giggle on occasion with her 'spooky' stories…. that is, until she turned up that particular day and said she had been to her spiritualist church and there was a visiting medium in attendance the week prior, and that she had a message for my mother …. We all sat there, trying not to giggle, waiting to hear what she had to say, bearing in mind she had not been in contact with my mother and knew nothing about those boots.   She told us that the medium spoke to her and said my brother was wanting to get a message to his mom, the message…. he had been to collect his boots!! You could have dropped a pin in that room.  You can bet your life, we weren't so keen to giggle at her antics in future!!

Quite a few years after those series of events at that house, I found myself at the centre of a spooky mystery or two!! I have a boyfriend by now and was around 16 at the time, said boyfriend was having his car resprayed by my father in the paint shop up the yard, behind the house. We were working on the car, masking it all up ready for my dad to spray the next morning. It was pitch dark, it being a winters' evening, so we had the lights on in the garage to see what we were doing, it was a long and painful process as that particular boyfriend was a perfectionist, oh the agony, I nearly masked his bloody mouth up after about half an hour!

Eventually, we were nearly finished, we had stopped what we were doing and, as he was a smoker, had stopped for him to have a cigarette. I was looking over the car, making sure the masking tape was perfect for 'his knibbs' when I heard my dad coming up the yard, I presumed to check on our progress. The heavy footsteps could be heard from about 75 feet away as the night was quiet and slightly misty so the sound carried up to us. We both stood there waiting for my dad to come into view, we waited, the footsteps got closer and closer, I couldn't see anyone at all, I wasn't afraid, just perplexed. Those damn footsteps kept on coming, right up to about 2 feet in front of me, the light from the paint shop reached out well into the yard, however, there was NOBODY there, I just stood there dumfounded, my boyfriend swore heatedly, (I learned a few new words that night!!) Neither of us knew how to react, or what we were facing, there was nothing there! We were just discussing what the hell had just happened, when we heard more footsteps, this time we were on high alert, looking into the darkness, waiting to see what was in store for us now, thankfully, this time it was my dad, I was never so pleased to see anyone in my life!! We told him about what had happened, and he was really laid back, said it had happened to him many times when he was working up the yard late at night doing some rush job or another, why he had never thought to mention this nugget of information one can only guess!!

My mother was also party to this startling news too, I found that out when I told her later that night, how in the heck do these people keep such shocking news to themselves?? I lived in a house where a ghost wandered aimlessly about in the night, didn't they think I wanted to know this news?? Well, thinking about it, no, I didn't want to know this news, I never wanted to know that something otherworldly was roaming around whilst I was sleeping!

This was probably the first paranormal thing that ever happened to me personally and fuelled an interest in the subject that has grown over the years. About a year after all this happened, one more thing happened inside that house and directly to me. I was having a major row with my mother, we were literally having a shouting match, God alone knows what it was about, but it was pretty heated, that I do remember. I stormed out of the kitchen and headed through the lounge to the bottom of the stairs, fully intent on stomping loudly up the stairs in a typical teenage fashion, on my way through the lounge, which was typically a country living room with big fire place and brass companion set in the fireplace. As I stomped huffily past the fireplace, the companion set suddenly rattled very violently, the noise was so loud, it stopped me in my tracks. I stood there dumbly looking at the companion set, wondering what the hell was going on. After a few moments, I managed to gather myself and made my way up to my bedroom where I was able to sit down and think about what it all meant.

I concluded that it may have been my brother trying to stop the arguing, he was always a bit of a peacemaker. I certainly shut me up that's for sure and there's not much that can do that!

This is Mill House that has been described in previous paragraphs, it was originally a two up, two down, with its very own stream running through the kitchen! My dad built the house without much help, he did all the drainage, electrics, plumbing, roofing etc, that was back in the days when you could do everything yourself! If you look over the large gate you can see the apex roof of the brick building that I was stood in with my boyfriend, when we had a visit with the unknown! The far chimney on the main house is the one that was hit by lightning, producing the Ball Lightning. All in all, a really historic, interesting place. My brother got killed about 2 miles up the road, and is buried half a mile down the road

***

A few months after these events, our village was rocked
with the sudden death of a stable boy, Derek, at our local
racing stables, he had been finishing off for the day, doing
the afternoon feeds, making sure all the horses had water,
feed and their stables were clean for the night ahead. He
went to the grain store and found there was not enough for
the evening feed, and made a decision that ended his life.
There was a massive grain silo on the farm next door, he
decided to climb up the outside of the silo and when he got
to the top, he found he couldn't reach the grain with the
bucket he had with him, so he decided to drop down on top
of the grain, get his bucket full and climb back out.
Sadly, he hadn't taken into account the 'quick sand' effect
of all that grain and he very quickly began to sink in, he
fought hard to keep his head out of the grain, he shouted
and screamed for help. Our local Landlord heard his cries,
he ran down to the silo and very quickly realised what had
happened, he grabbed a length of rope and climbed quickly
to the top, tying himself off, he jumped in and attempted a
rescue. Sadly, although he fought to pull Derek out, he

couldn't pull against the 'tow' of the grain, he managed to tie the rope around a hand and climbed back up the rope himself and shouted for more help. A few more of the villagers had realised what was happening by now and were on their way up the silo. It was all too late for poor Derek, he was already dead, his mouth, nose, eyes and ears being full of grain. Gave our poor Landlord, Ted, nightmares for years to come!

Some 6 months after these events, myself and my brother and a few other young people were at our house and for some stupid reason we decided that our entertainment for the evening would be greatly improved with the addition of an upturned mirror, some ABC cards and a couple of 'Yes/No' cards….in other words, a Ouija board!! My mom was out with my dad at the time, as she would have literally skinned us alive if she knew what we were up to, especially as my elder brother had been killed in an accident a couple of years before, along with his best friend in a separate accident a couple of weeks later, and also my aunt, that October and also a couple others in local villages, 1973 was a VERY bad year for deaths locally….

and now another death in the village, we were on our toes, keeping an eye out for their car coming back!!

We got ourselves all set up, gave the mirror a final polish for good luck and laid out the cards, we chose a glass and turned all the lights off, lighting a few candles around the room, for atmosphere you understand!! We all sat there, trying not to laugh, or run in my case!

My brother appointed himself as 'master of ceremonies' and began asking that age old question 'Is anyone there?'. There were stifled giggles around the table, we were all a bit terrified. He asked again, and a couple of more times, nothing was happening. We were just about to give up, much to my relief. All of a sudden, the glass started to move, I was convinced someone was moving it. We all took it in turns to take our fingers off the glass, just to prove that nobody was in fact moving the thing! When we were relatively confident that we had indeed 'made contact', my brother began asking questions, fully expecting, and probably hoping, that it was our big brother who had died a couple of years before. It wasn't him, the glass was pretty tentative in its' movements for a while, then got much bolder, and it eventually spelled out the name 'Derek', our hapless stable boy. Well by now, I was absolutely convinced someone must be moving the bloody glass, this couldn't be real…could it??

Again, each and every person slowly, one by one, took their fingers off the glass, I was last, and was absolutely terrified when the damn thing carried on moving with just my finger on it, only for a short distance, but enough to prove to me that it was under some 'other worldly' power! 'Derek' answered a few questions put by my brother, which proved further that it was actually him. He stated that he was bloody furious with himself for being so stupid and wanted to apologise to Ted for frightening the life out of him, which I thought was rather nice. We didn't have much time for any more questions, as someone shouted that there was a car coming up the lane, (we lived about a mile outside the village and cars were a rarity in those days). We packed up at lightning speed, turned on the lights and tuned in the TV to something boring, leaping into our seats, and trying to make it look like we had been there for hours. Sweat breaking out on our collective foreheads, as we knew how my mother felt about Ouija board. We were never more relieved than when that car slowly sailed past our house and off up the lane, it wasn't them! We have packed everything away by then so didn't really feel like getting it all out again, we felt we had a lucky escape that time! My brother did approach Ted, the landlord of our local pub with the news he had for him, swearing him to say nothing to our mother, or we were all dead! Ted promised to say nothing, he didn't really believe what he was told anyway just thought it was us kids being stupid!

A year or so after these events, my brother caused a few grey hairs on both parents, when, one day he came sheepishly into the kitchen and asked if he could borrow the tractor to tow a car out of the hedge. My dad was immediately on point and wanted to know what car, where??
We had managed to get an old car started, and with the help of some petrol we siphoned off some of the other scrap cars we had about the place, we managed to get this old banger going and we were driving it around the field opposite the house. My brother, not content with going around and around, that was way too boring for him. No,

he decided he was going to try turning the car over, after wedging a brick on the accelerator and throwing himself out of course, the poor old car managed six rolls before coming to a halt. This was good, but not good enough for him.

There was a large bank at the end of the field, with a stand of tall trees below, my brother decided it would be great if the car could be made to go fast enough to take off from the bank and clear the trees!! He began his run from the top of the field, heading down, gaining speed, again he wedged the brick on the accelerator, timed it just right and threw himself out of the car. That poor car hurtled down the field getting faster and faster, the engine was screaming by the time it hit the bank. It took off like a flying brick, not very aerodynamic, nor indeed high enough to clear the trees, no, instead it hit the trees about two thirds of the way up. They swayed alarmingly and almost catapulted the car back at us, but we were saved by a large branch which somehow snagged the car and kept it stuck in the trees, swaying about in the breeze. It was at this point that my brother headed over to the house and made his plea for the tractor. Needless to say, when my dad saw the new 'tree decoration' we were banned from driving any old bangers for a long while after that.

We did manage to persuade my dad to let us use a very old, and very slow scooter, which was fun, or would have been had someone bothered to show me how to stop the bloody thing, I had to run it into a bramble bush in order to come to a halt, very scratched, not very impressed. I have never liked two wheels to this day!

I much preferred the four legs of my pony, he was an Appaloosa, with a spotty bottom and I loved him. I used to spend hours grooming and riding out with my friends. They were very happy days in my childhood, could have been slightly happier had (some) of the local villagers not treated us like Gypsy's or Tinkers. They were always happy enough for my dad to tow them out of the mess they had gotten themselves into and repair their cars, but we were never raised above serfdom in their eyes!!

We used to welcome the Romanies that travelled around the area, like swallows, they would turn up every year around the same time, the two that stick in the mind are the Butlers and the Woodwards, both lovely familes, never left any mess, never caused us any concerns at all, just lovely families who kept themselves to themselves. They always parked in a large gateway to the field opposite our house. Eb Woodward was such a kind man, when my brother died, Eb found out at the site he was staying on in London and jumped into his van and drove all the way to our house to tell my parents how sorry he was, he bought mom some hand-made pegs, a few of which I still have to this day. There's not many folks who would go to those lengths just to show respect, a gentleman indeed!

In fact, my own grandmother was the opposite end of the scale to Eb, she received the telegram my mother sent her, (about my brother dying), didn't reply and even hid it from my grandfather and he didn't find out for nearly a month, when he accidentally came across it in some paperwork! Bless him, he did no more than determined he was going to get to us somehow, my grandmother (The Cow!), kept him short of money, and he didn't have a car, so he did the only thing he could think of, he set off to walk, from Worcester to our house near Twycross in Leicestershire, miles and miles, he was 78 at the time. When he got around 20 miles away, he found a phone box and made a reverse charge call to my mom as he just couldn't walk any further. She jumped in the car and fetched him, not quite believing what she was being told about her own mother!! What's that old saying again? 'You can choose your friends, but not your family'… never truer than with my grandmother, never, ever, remember her making any fuss of us kids, never had cards, presents or any single word of encouragement from that woman.

She lived until she was 96 despite smoking 40 a day, my mother always said that she was too evil to die!

# Supernatural or Super Natural?

Many years ago, during a huge storm that brought down power lines, trees and blocked roads, my family were living in the house described in the previous chapters, it had been renovated by now and was a four-bedroom house with coal fires in each of the lounges. Everyone was sat around the fire, huddled against the storm, it had become quite hair raising and loud, we were all a bit jumpy and excited by the thunder, which was enough to rattle the teeth in your head!

Suddenly there was an almighty crack, it sounded like the roof was coming in, we all leaped up in the air, my dad was just about ready to run outside to see what damage had been done, when the fire changed colour, from red to blue and green, it started sparkling, spitting and became almost alive. With that, we all stopped our headlong rush to find out what had occurred and gave the fire our full attention. Almost immediately an extremely bright, white orb came floating, presumably down the chimney, as we hadn't got a clue where else it could have come from and floated, fizzing and popping into the room. We were all transfixed by the sight of this other worldly thing, it was about as big as a cricket ball and glowed angrily, fizzing and crackling in a most alarming way. My mother let out a blood curdling scream, and 'boy' could she scream! 'Nobody move, stand perfectly still' she screeched. We did as we were told as this 'thing' fizzed and floated around the room. It seemed like ages it was floating around, but it could only have been seconds, it bobbed around by the fireplace and headed up towards the ceiling, with us all sat, stood or in various poses frozen with fascination at this most unusual sight. It was bobbing around the ceiling for a couple of seconds, then, suddenly, blinked out and was gone! What the hell just happened? We all just stood there for a second or two, almost transfixed, when there came a very loud clatter on the front door. We all nearly jumped right out of our skin, a neighbour was knocking as he had seen the lightning strike the house and thought the chimney might be on fire! This intrusion got us all moving again and we shared our story of the 'orb' with him, he, being of old country stock, like my parents, was of the

opinion that we had been visited by 'Ball Lightning'.
Nowadays, there are people who will tell you that it
doesn't exist, well, I can tell you I have seen it, heard it,
felt it (it made all the hair on my body stand on end!) and
most unusual of all 'smelled it', it was a weird metallic,
burning smell, all very odd!!

A year or so before this event, I remember another storm
that visited our little village. The 'big storm' as it became
known locally (aren't they all??) took down trees, power
lines, caused floods and all manner of chaos. Didn't stop
me from heading off down the village to see what trouble I
could get up to you understand, not a lot would keep me
indoors back then!

After a couple of hours with my friends, roaming round,
getting soaked and generally 'dossing about', I decided it
was time to head home as by now it was getting dark and if
I left it much later, it would be totally dark and my dad
would be out on the war path looking for me! I started to
run back up the lane, I always ran up that lane in those
days, it was long, dark and creepy and I never wanted to
hang about. There were no street lights back in those days.

I got about half way back home, when I heard crackling, saw sparks flying across the road and then noticed that the power line was down. Only it wasn't just lying there, it was whipping about like a snake on 'E's!! I started to walk up to it and it was almost like it 'knew' I was there, it whipped around and landed about a foot in front of my feet, snapping, sparking and crackling. I moved to the side and it moved again. I tried this a few times and was beginning to panic, I convinced myself that this damn power line was alive and after my blood. I was about to give up and head back into the village to summon help, when I looked again and saw that where the line had come down, it was pinned by a fallen tree, I decided to take my chance, and ran, leaped upon the fallen tree and hopped off the other side, then ran like stink back home. I was never more please to get back home. My dad arranged for the line to be repaired, and when the chaps came to do the job, I went to talk to them, I told my story of the 'mad snake' and they were utterly shocked that I had just jumped over it. They said I was 'bloody mad' ….charming!!

# Bishops Nympton – Devon

An old friend, whom I shall call Dave, was renting a cottage in the village a good few years ago, he had been living there about 3 weeks when myself and hubby went down for a visit and look the new place over, and most importantly of all, check out the local pub!

We arrived early and had to sit in the car waiting for him to turn up for nearly an hour, it was a dark winter's afternoon, so the house looked old and spooky before we even entered it. After we dropped off our bags we went to the local pub and spent a good couple of hours there, then it was back to the house for more drinks and maybe a little food. By now it was around 10pm and we all sat round talking and laughing. A few minutes past 10, we were asked to listen quietly….

We all sat there expectantly, waiting for whatever it was we were supposed to be listening for, however, nothing could have prepared us for what we did hear!! At approximately 10.10pm, we heard footsteps upstairs, they were very distinct, then a door in the room directly above our heads creaked open, creaked closed again, and the footsteps crossed the room to towards the window! The light fitting above our heads actually began to swing back and forth with the movement of the floor! We sat there transfixed, what in the heck?? 'Who is upstairs??' I asked, trying to remember if I had been told there was someone else in the house.

Our host just laughed, he said this routine happened every night at 10.10pm, if they ('they' being Dave and his girlfriend), were tired, they would wait until the 'ghost had walked' before going to bed, as their bedroom just happened to be the one the ghost walked through!! I would have crapped myself if that had happened to me whilst I as in that flaming bed!

A short time later my hubby decided he needed to take a leak, Dave failed to point out that there was actually a perfectly serviceable toilet downstairs and directed my hubby to the one upstairs, in the next room to the one we had just heard the footsteps in!! Still, the lights were all on, it would be fine….

Hubby went into the bathroom, a little reluctantly it had to be said, all the lights were blazing. As soon as the door was firmly closed, Dave hurtled up the stairs as quietly as he could, ran into the bedroom, pulled a sheet off his bed, threw it over his head and turned off the landing light to wait for the poor wretch in the toilet! Meanwhile, my hubby had heard a creaking floorboard outside the bathroom, very reluctantly he slowly creaked opened the door, only to find the landing lights were out, and there stood right in front of him, a vision in white, groaning and moaning, I think the loud resonant fart gave it away, but by then hubby was beyond sense, he was terrified out of his wits! The girly screech that emanated from him made me question his manliness for weeks!! He let out a blood curdling howl and leapt down the stairs, quite literally missing almost every step! Dave, meanwhile was in a heap, laughing his head off, this, he decided was the best thing he had ever done!

Hubby meanwhile was trying to lever his battered and bruised carcass off the flagstone floor at the bottom of the stairs…… me?  Oh, I was in a fit of giggles for at least an hour, I am nothing if not supportive!!

We stayed there for the next two nights, both of which we heard those footsteps, the creaking door and the march across the bedroom, the footsteps fading out as they reached the window…. It was a classic case of a 'residual haunting' I have since found out!!  Hubby??  Yes, he did start speaking to me again, pretty quickly, says volumes for his ability to forgive!!

# The Durham Experience

Our friend, 'Dave' was again involved in this incident, which occurred in a house he and some friends were renovating a few years ago.

The house in question was built around the turn of the century and was a three-storey town house in Durham. It was in a terrible state, needed completely gutting and renovating. The boys arrived after a very long drive in a battered Transit van that was also on its' last legs. They spent a fruitless hour trying to find a cheap bed and breakfast before heading over to the house in question.

Having failed to find somewhere to stay, they decided to camp out inside the house, there was running water and a couple of the rooms were just about habitable. They made themselves comfortable and began knocking bits off the house, after half a day's work, it was getting dark, and with no electricity they decided to head off to the local pub for something to eat and drink. After a couple of hours, they all headed back to the house and having bought a couple of 'smelly' candles from a local shop, they were the only kind they could find, they settled down to sleep. The first night went quietly, they all had a skin full of ale, so weren't going to wake, even if the place had fallen down!

The second day, they continued the demolition job and again headed off to the pub for some food, they decided not to drink too much the second night as they all felt pretty rough after the previous night and wanted to be up early to get on with the job. Their toilet left something to be desired, it was a bucket in the corner of the room, as no-one wanted to have to get up and go downstairs and outside in the dark, where the only other working toilet could be found, besides, the spiders in there had hobnail boots on – in other words, they were freaking massive and would probably have dragged a small child in for a snack! Nobody fancied that!

When Dave woke in the early hours for a 'leak' he noticed the door to the room was open, it was cold so he closed it again, did what he woke up for and settled back down to sleep. When he woke again in the morning, the door was again open, he assumed one of the others had opened it and thought no more about it. They went about their business that day and repeated the pub visit later on. They all went back to settle down for sleep and Dave asked that no-one leave the door open if they went out, as it was cold.

They all went to sleep without too much trouble, in the early hours, Dave heard someone 'kick the bucket' and he stifled a giggle, hoping they hadn't spilled the contents. He lay there for a few seconds and decided that he too needed a leak, he got up, and was surprised that everyone else seemed to be fast asleep, and the door was wide open again! He grumbled to himself, closed the door, relieved himself and lay back down to sleep. Within a few minutes he heard a noise, some sort of shuffling, then the door opened again. He sat up, thinking he had caught the culprit who kept leaving the flaming door open, but the room was quiet, and everyone else was breathing deeply and obviously fast asleep. He thought he must have been dreaming, closed the door again and tried to settle down to sleep. Within about 5 minutes he could clearly hear someone coming up the stairs, their being on the first floor.

He sat bolt upright and waited, thinking there must be a tramp in the place, the door opened once again, and he strained to see who it was, couldn't see a thing, so flicked his lighter on to get a better look, there was no-one there! By now, the others were beginning to wake up with all the noise of the steps, rubbing their eyes and wondering what was going on.

Dave shot up and ran to the door, convinced he was going to find someone in the hallway or heading down the stairs, there was nobody at all, and everything was quiet, the others had a laugh at him and said he had been dreaming. He knew he hadn't but took the banter good naturedly. The next day they got on with the job at hand and after the visit to the pub, the landlord of whom couldn't believe his luck, 5 lads eating and drinking like it was going out of fashion every night of the week, he must have been planning a week in Ibiza based on this lot!

When they got back to the house, Dave decided to put a stop to the door opening saga once and for all, he got a couple of six-inch nails and banged them through the door into the door jamb so that nobody could open it until they got up in the morning, he thought he had it sussed this time!!  Well, you know what thought did???

Around 2 am, they all awoke to stomping and banging, they all sat bolt upright and lit their candles quickly, and watched in horror as someone or something banged and banged on the door, the jam was beginning to crack, Dave jumped up and using the claw hammer, yanked out the two nails and the door flew open hitting him as it did.  They all ran out into the hall in their underpants (what a sight that must have been!!), fully expecting to find the culprit and give them a piece of their minds, but, after running around and around the house, several times, they could find no-one.  The boys were thoroughly put out, but were still convinced this was a flesh and blood person and they were going to devise a plan to catch the 'bugger' the next night!

The following day, they worked as normal, went to the pub as normal, (bet the landlord was relieved!), then started working out their plan for the night.  They made sure the front door was fully bolted, all the windows shut and secure.  They searched the house whilst it was still light enough to see, to make sure there was nobody hiding in any of the nooks and crannies. They bought a small pack of flour and sprinkled it all over the place, paying particular attention to the stairs and landing area. This so they could track the intruder to where they came in and where they left. They had even gone to the trouble of getting themselves several cheap torches, so they would have instant light in order to chase down the culprit. The door was again nailed shut, with a single nail this time for a fast response, and they all settled down, trying to get some sleep, but keeping a 'weather eye' out for anything unusual.

In the early hours, there was again a commotion on the landing, the door was being pushed and banged, they all leapt up and grabbed their torches determined this time they were going to catch someone!! Dave flew to the door, levered out the single nail, they were all ready when the door flew open, the torches were all aimed at the doorway, but the doorway and landing were completely empty, they were utterly perplexed, nobody could have got away that quickly. They stood there for a second or two gathering their wits, when it was quickly noticed that there were no marks in the flour, what the hell??? They are utterly spooked now, knowing for sure this was no 'normal' person. They quietly decided amongst themselves that they actually did'nt need to search the house in the dark with an invisible force wandering around and huddled together in the room until it got light. When it did get light, they checked out the whole place and there were no marks in the flour anywhere in the house!

They decided that morning that maybe a hotel would be in order, even if it did cost a fortune, none of them were willing to spend another night in that place!!

# Austrey House

This was a small hotel owned by my parents in a small town on the West Coast of England, called Weston-super-Mare. My mother dubbed the place 'Euston St Station' as it was pretty 'lively' even for our family who have lived in a few spooky places in the past, this place took the biscuit!

We moved there in December of 1979 and almost straight away it became obvious there was something 'odd' about the place! You couldn't walk down the stairs without looking behind you, it always felt like someone was watching you, you could almost feel the 'eyes' boring into the back of your head, it was very unsettling!

It was just mom and myself who moved in at first, with my dad joining us a few weeks later, by then, we were getting used to the place and the rooms that felt 'uncomfortable'.

I was sleeping at the very top of the house at the back in a small bedroom with a wonky floor – in fact, the whole upstairs had the 'funhouse' effect with the floors to varying degrees, one of the rooms you actually felt like you were walking downhill just crossing the room! I never felt comfortable in that room, in fact I moved out and into a room downstairs in very short order, I just couldn't go to sleep with my back to the door, it felt horrible trying to do so, my spine would prickle with anticipation, it was a horrid room! It was only about 6 months later that my mother, with her twisted sense of humour admitted to me that when she slept in that room (we played 'musical rooms' when we first moved in!), she awoke in the early hours and felt tiny feet running all over the damn bed!! I am so glad she didn't tell me that before I slept in there for a week! Not!!

The downstairs had its' own spooky residents too, my boyfriend used to stay occasionally and slept in the lounge on the sofa-bed. My mother slept in the room next to that and one night she got up to relieve herself, on the way down the long hallway towards the toilet she could see into the kitchen in the moonlight and could see (who she thought was) my boyfriend leaning on his elbows on the kitchen sink looking out of the window. Having finished with her toilet, she decided that as my boyfriend was in the kitchen, she would go into the lounge and have a look out onto the street as was her habit.  She walked into the lounge and was a little shocked to see my boyfriend sound asleep, she thought he must have moved pretty quickly, but turned around and headed back into the hallway towards her own room, not wishing to disturb him.  She nearly dropped when she came into the hall proper and saw that same visage – the 'person' was still leaning, elbows on the sink, looking out of the window, backlit by the moon.  My mother was not easily spooked, but that nearly made her faint, she went quietly back into her bedroom, locked the door firmly and stayed there until it was light (my dad had still not moved in at this point).  She was telling me about this in the morning, and was really quite startled by it, my dad arrived later that day, she felt a lot better having someone else permanently sharing her room after that! What he didn't tell her for a few years was that, a few weeks after moving into that room, he awoke to an awful rasping noise and opened his eyes to find an old woman leaning over the bed staring at him.  I asked him what he did, he said 'nothing, what could I do, I just closed my eyes and asked her silently to go away, then turned over and cuddled into your mother and went back to sleep'!! Balls of steel that man!

A year or so later, yes, we were still there!  I was having a bit of an argument with my mother in the kitchen, it was lunchtime and I had given her my considered opinion, turned to walk out of the back door, when a bunch of tea towels came flying at me!  I turned to my mother and asked her why she had thrown them at me?  She just stood there, mouth gaping, I again asked why she had thrown them, she pointed out that she was in the wrong direction and the tea towels had come from the other direction, and 'no' she hadn't thrown them!!  I saw the truth in this and we immediately forgot our argument and wondered what the heck was going on!

My 21st birthday was looming and we arranged for loads of family to stay, we had a lovely time, few drinks, great food, it was fun.  My friend and her boyfriend stayed the night in the lounge, again on the sofa-bed. I am a natural early riser, so I said I would make sure they were up in the morning as the boyfriend needed to get to work for 7am. (why does it always sound so easy to do when you have had too much to drink?), I duly dragged myself out of seven layers of drink induced sleep, staggered downstairs, and got them both up. Whilst they were dressing I went down the hallway into the kitchen and got the kettle on and busied myself making them and myself a much-needed cup of tea. When the kettle boiled I was just pouring the water into the cups, suddenly I felt all my hair stand on end and a massive wolf whistle was blown into my ear, I actually felt the wind off it. My drink laced brain was startled, but I was sufficiently drunk enough not to feel real fear. I actually told myself I had been dreaming and carried on making the tea, it was only when I got back to the lounge, tea in hand when they both turned to me and asked who I had been whistling at, that I actually started feeling a little frightened!! That bloody whistle had really happened, the more I thought about it, the more unsettled I felt. I then remembered back to my mother saying she had seen a 'youngish man leaning on the kitchen sink, looking out of the window' and realised that is who that must have been!!

We had several guests who stayed in that place who left quickly after booking for a week, they would be very tight lipped and would make up some excuse or other, only one family actually came out and said that they had been disturbed by something unseen! They had heard someone stomping round the room and turning the taps off and on in the bathroom, this happened to them twice in their weeks' stay, however they didn't want to change rooms and weren't entirely upset by it, they just thought it was quite exciting!! Some people are just plain daft methinks!!

A couple of guests gave us all reason to experience a moment's hesitation at the choice of business we ran. The first was a middle aged, rather portly, greying gentleman who had one of the rooms at the top of the house for a week. He seemed perfectly 'normal' when he booked in, even jovial and chatty. He requested an extra towel, which my mother took up to him later on that evening. She knocked on the door and he called for her to 'come in'. When she opened the door she was totally taken aback to see this, previously, so normal gent, dressed in a very short, baby doll, frilly green nightie!! She quickly dropped the towel on the bed and made a sharp exit, eyes popping like corks! I don't know how I managed to keep a straight face when I serve that chaps breakfast for a week, but somehow I did, you just never know who you have in your house!! At least this one seemed harmless enough, the next was a different kettle of fish!

Another time, and another chap, this one booked in for a 2 night stay, all seemed quite normal, he did seem a bit 'jumpy' to me, but nothing enough to raise suspicion. It wasn't until after he had left that we had a visit from the Police. They were very interested in the chap who had checked out that morning. There were lots of questions, then they dropped the bombshell… there had been a murder in a nearby town, a woman had been strangled, her body had been left in her house and a relative had found it when they went to investigate why she was incommunicado!
Turned out that 'Mr Jumpy' was actually wanted for murder, what was worse, he was arrested a few days later on the south coast and tried for that murder and is currently

at 'Her Majesty's Pleasure'… as I said before, you just never knew who you were letting in your house!

# 'Sid the Spectre'

By now I had a home of my own and 2 gorgeous kids, Josh and Charlotte, they were both under 5 at the time. Charlotte was very unsettled and not sleeping well in our new house. We later found out that she was Autistic and had both a severe learning delay and severe speech delay, but this all happened about a year before that nightmare hit us!

Josh was already in his own bed, Charlotte kept crying and trying to climb out of her cot, she was very restless some nights, not so others, so you couldn't put it down to routine, which always remained the same. We started to keep an eye on what she was eating, what was happening before bed, what type of day she'd had, all the usual stuff.

A couple of times during the night we had been woken up by an awful stink of poo, even my hubby Dennis woke up, which believe me, is a bit of a miracle in itself!! I used to get up at the run, convinced that one of them had done something awful in bed, I would check on both, who on each occasion would be fast asleep, I even checked on my Dad, who lived with us, just in case he was ill, nothing, all was normal and everyone sleeping peacefully, except of course yours truly. What was more disturbing was that, more often than not, as soon as I stood up, I would feel extremely dizzy, it would literally feel like I was stood on the deck of a ship in a hurricane. I would bounce off the walls trying to get out of the room and find out what was going on. I even went to the doctors and he said I had 'Labrynthitis', an inflammation of the inner ear, and that I would probably get it again and again. Well, you know what, I never had it again since the day we left that house!

One morning Josh was eating his breakfast, he was about 3 at the time, when he said 'Mom, can you tell that old man to stop coming in my room', well you can imagine the scene, we were all in the middle of breakfast, pouring tea, spreading butter on toast etc, when Josh drops this bombshell, everyone came to a halt, it was like someone had pressed the pause button! 'What old man', say's I, not actually wanting to hear. 'What does he look like, do you mean granddad?' I said hopefully, (who lived with us at the time). 'No, it's not granddad, it's another old man and he keeps coming in my room and waking me up'.

You could hear a pin drop in that kitchen, none of us knew what to say, I managed to promise Josh I would have a very stern talk with this 'old man' and ask him to stop immediately, Josh was unfazed and carried on eating as if it was a normal day. Dennis, Dad and I just kept giving each other meaningful looks!!

When Josh was in playgroup later in the day and Charlotte was taking a nap I rather bravely went upstairs and decided that if there were some sort of paranormal happenings going on, I for one was not going to have any of it. I marched up and down through the bedrooms and the landing reading the riot act to 'Spectral Sid' as we had nicknamed said 'old man'. I had a real go as if I was talking to a real person, honest to God, you would have had me committed if you had seen me!

Life seemed to return to normal and Josh didn't mention 'Sid' again, 'job done' I thought, that telling off did the trick! There didn't seem to be anything going on in our house prior to this, no bumps, bangs, footsteps etc, it all felt quite normal and safe so I wasn't frightened at all. In fact, it was all a bit of a lark, I told a couple of mum's who were round having a coffee one day about Josh's midnight visitor, and one of them suggested using Sage to cleanse the house, well that was it, straight into the kitchen, and a box of Sage & Onion stuffing was liberated from the cupboard, and laughing like the demented, I wandered round threatening to stuff 'Spectral Sid' if he showed his face in my house again!

A couple of weeks of peace later and we were again woken up by the horrible smell, I again got up thinking it was one of my little stink bombs, I was once again really dizzy to the point of bouncing off walls. I stepped out of our bedroom and noticed that the smell was no longer there, 'odd' I thought, 'where's that gone?'. I stood on the landing swaying about for a few seconds just listening, nothing, not a sound. I went back into our bedroom, only to be met by the smell again. I know what you are thinking, Dennis + curry = stink, yes, so did I, to start with, but it wasn't that type of smell, it was like raw sewage, literally like someone had crapped all over the carpet then rubbed it in – I should know, I had Charlotte!! (Also, it happened one night when Dennis was on nights and not even there!) After a few moments the smell went and all returned to normal. This happened several more times during the next few weeks, the horrible smell, the nasty dizziness. It was all very odd and unsettling.

One morning I was chatting to my friend on the phone in the hall, it was very early, about 6.45am, we both had small children and were up at all sorts of silly hours, so regularly chatted early. My dad was still in bed as he had been ill, Josh was also still asleep. Dennis was at work. It was only myself and Charlotte up, she was in the lounge lining up cars, bless!

I was looking out of the front window chatting away and heard my Dad coming down the stairs, all wheezy, slow steps, poor old thing I thought, I'll go and make him a cup of tea in a minute. My friend and I were laughing about the noise the stairs made, they were possibly the squeakiest, creakiest stairs you had ever heard, and she could even hear the noise over the phone!! I was stood with my back to the stairs, I could easily have turned around to speak to my 'dad' however, I couldn't tell you, to this day, why I didn't, I just felt compelled to continue the conversation and keep looking out of the window in front of me.

Anyway, we finished the call and arranged to meet at the park with the children later in the day and I went off to find dad and make him a cup of tea. I called him as I walked into the kitchen, not there, I thought he's maybe in the toilet at the back of the house, waited a few moments, nothing, I went to check the toilet, he wasn't there. I was becoming a bit alarmed, I had been round the ground floor twice, and I could not find him, where the heck was he…. I knew he'd come down, both myself and my friend had heard him. I went around again, still nothing, then I went upstairs and into his bedroom, he was still in bed, fast asleep, ditto Josh!! What the hell just happened???? I rang back my friend and asked her to confirm that she had definitely heard the stairs going just to make sure I wasn't going completely mad. She confirmed that, yes, she had definitely heard the stairs, she had even heard the wheezing!! Jeez, I went all cold!! Spectral Sid had struck again!!

After this, the smell and the dizzy spells started to become a regular thing, never could find a cause, it wasn't until I saw one of these paranormal shows a couple of years later that I put the two together, Sid was the smell, and may even have been responsible for the awful dizziness! I also found that if I took a photograph in that downstairs hall, which I did quite a lot, I used to take photos of my kids weekly in those days; there was always a red mist in any that were taken at the bottom of those stairs. You could take a photo there, mist included, go into the lounge take another, no mist, back into the hall, there it was again, I have quite a few pictures of red mist, again, I didn't put that down to 'Sid' until a couple of years later! Here are a couple of those photos…

What finally put the mockers on that house and made us reach for the Estate Agents number was one particular morning when I was stood in the kitchen and Dennis came up behind me and stood really close, nothing unusual there, he does that quite a lot, usually includes a kiss and cuddle, so I wasn't worried, until I turned around to speak to him and he wasn't there, there was nobody there!

Get that 'For Sale' board NOW!

*This is a photo of my dad and Josh at the back of that house, the events   described above all happened here.*

# Mom

I will never forget the lead up to losing my mom, for nearly two months I just simply stopped sleeping, there was nothing I could do to get to sleep, my mind was whizzing round and round like a fruit machine.  I got so desperate for a decent kip, I even went to the doctors and asked for sleeping tablets, but she wouldn't give me any, so it was the chemist and the next best thing, 'Kalms', which didn't really help either.  I remember one night going down to the kitchen in the wee small hours, standing by the sink eyeing up a carving knife and wondering what it would be like to plunge it into my chest, I was that delusional and zonked out from not sleeping.  I was trying to hold down a full-time job in Bristol at the time, and it was absolute hell.  I swear that night when I reached that lowest of the low, I saw myself, stood in front of myself in that kitchen, it was the weirdest thing ever, probably the result of my addled brain, but at the time, it felt real!!

I also became strangely 'psychic' too, it was really odd. I also had an almost permanent feeling that something was about to happen, it was exhausting. I remember telling someone at work that I was convinced something bad was going to happen. One evening when I was about to leave work for the bus home, I remember looking at the few odd bits of change I kept in my pen holder at work, and thinking, 'you had better take that for when the bus breaks down on the way home, you'll need something for the phone', not too many mobiles in those days…1995!! The darnedest thing happened, before we even got all the way up the Long Ashton Bypass, the bloody bus broke down, all the hairs on the back of my neck stood right on end!! About a week later, I had really odd dream that three men were crawling around on the floor of the office I worked in, in the dark, lighting up matches, it was pretty surreal and I couldn't think where that had come from, that is until

I got into work the next day and found that we had been broken into the previous night, most of the computers had been pinched, and there were spent matches all over the floor, the police surmised that the robbers had used matches to see what they were doing when unplugging the computers! I was flabbergasted to say the least! The police were more than a little suspicious when I said that there were three of them and they lowered the stuff out of the window at the back of the office to a waiting van, cos I hadn't even been back there yet, and that's exactly what had happened!! The police gave me some very funny looks after that, kept looking at me as if I was some kind of weirdo, well, actually I pretty much was!

There were a few other little things that I knew before they happened, it wasn't at all spooky or frightening, it was just a 'knowing', just like you know the route home, it didn't seem at all odd, until after those events, then I really wondered what the heck was going on!

The end of April saw me getting really quite ill with all the sleeplessness, I was getting to the end of my tether, I still had the awful feeling that something dreadful was going to happen, this had been going on for nearly two months by now and was really getting me down. I didn't tell my mom or dad, or even my hubby as I couldn't actually vocalise how I was feeling as it would have sounded bloody mad! Mom and Dad were due on holiday on 3rd May, they were going to fly out to Malta for a two-week holiday and I was really starting to think something awful was going to happen to either one of them, I really didn't want them getting on that plane, but how do you tell someone you don't want them getting on a plane for a lovely holiday without sounding like a complete nutter?? My hubby and I went for Sunday lunch with the both of them and I remember feeling that I really didn't want to leave, I mean I REALLY didn't want to leave, I kept putting it off, in the end my hubby insisted we go as we were supposed to be meeting friends for a drink and it was a workday the next day. I remember leaving the house feeling terrible, I wanted to cry, I remember making eye contact with my mom when she came out to see us off, she asked me what was wrong, I couldn't say, how do you say to someone, I think you or dad might die?? As by now, I was convinced someone was going to die.

The Monday 1st May saw me sat at home in the early evening, I had just had a long conversation with my mom on the phone, I was due round the next afternoon to take their dog Sally to the kennels before they were due to fly on the Wednesday. She had not managed to speak to my brother who, as usual, was too busy leading his life to bother checking his answerphone! We ended the call and I went to sit and watch the TV whilst waiting for hubby to come home from work.

I sat there about an hour and a half and suddenly became seriously spooked, I was convinced there was someone in the room with me, I actually leaped up off the sofa and looked back at it, fully expecting to see someone sat there, it was that real!! As I was stood there, wondering what the hell that was, the phone rang, it was my Dad, all he could say was 'your moms' had an accident' and 'I've called the ambulance'. With that, I was in the car and on the way to their house which mercifully was only about 4 minutes away. I arrived just as the ambulance did, and they went upstairs to see my mom, as she was actually in the bathroom having just had a bath. Dad was stood outside the bathroom and the dog was running wild round the house, I managed to wrangle the dog into the kitchen and close the door, so that she didn't run out into the road as the front door was stood wide open. I ran upstairs to my dad and he was beside himself, he thought she was still alive as when he turned her over she breathed, later it became clear this was not the case, she had died instantly and the 'breath' was her lungs emptying themselves with the movement of her body. She had a Beri Aneurysm – which is a burst blood vessel in the brain, death is usually pretty quick after that, but not always, some people do recover either in degrees or indeed a near enough full recovery, it just depends upon the area of the brain that is damaged.

The next few days are a blur of mourning and sadness, organising a refund of their holiday money (thank goodness, they hadn't gotten on that plane, with a Beri Aneurysm it would have burst before 35,000 feet and that would have been terrible enough without the fact that my dad would have been on his own). The funeral was organised for Tuesday 8th May which was the anniversary to the day of my brothers' death in 1973 as if the day wasn't sad enough already, it was either that date or wait another week!

A couple of days after my mom died, I remember feeling a bizarre sense of relief, which sounds completely heartless to say the least, but I was actually sleeping again, and that awful sense of expectation had gone. I have never felt so odd, so out of sorts and so lost as I did in those first few weeks. Anyone who has lost a mom will know how that feels!

I don't remember much about the run up to the funeral, it was such a sad and sorry time, the actual day of the funeral went as expected and myself and my hubby went back to our house to sleep that night. We were just getting off to sleep when this arsehole who worked with my hubby decided at 12.30 at night, the night of the funeral, it would be a good time to phone up and talk about shite! Hubby went completely overboard and slammed the phone down, stomped off out of the bedroom, stating he was going around this dickheads house to give him a piece of his mind, he was tamping mad.  He came back into the bedroom and was ranting about what he intended to do to the dickhead, when all hell broke loose in the house, the doors all opened and slammed shut again, things flew off the windowsill, stuff in the hallway fell on the floor.  We were both startled, and I remember saying, 'that's mom wanting you to calm down and shut up and get back into bed', which he promptly did.  The rest of the night was quiet and nothing like that has ever happened since!!  I really do think it was my mom having her say!!

That was the last night we spent in our house, Dad was such a forlorn figure, we felt we couldn't leave him on his own, so we moved in with him and our family dynamics changed completely.  Dad remained with us throughout the next 15 years, being grandad to my kids, which he loved, teacher, dad, and general wonderful person until his death at the ripe old age of 80.

# Dad

As mentioned, Dad lived with us for 15 years after my mom died, he became the centre of our family, my son wouldn't bother coming to mom if he had a nightmare, he always went to grandad for a cuddle and sleep, Dad really did love being grandad!!

As he aged, he still worked right up until the age of 78, only part-time, but he loved to feel useful and was never lazy. Then one day, after a short illness, he was being examined by a hospital doctor, who, after running his hand over my dad's stomach, froze, did the sharp intake of breath you would normally expect from a builder with very bad news, then gave us the very bad news!! Dad had an Aortic Aneurism, that is a massive bulge in the wall of his Aorta, common in older gentlemen, in fact, each and every one of dad's 4 brothers had all died of the same thing!! Dad was booked in for emergency surgery, the aneurism was 12 centimetres, they get critical at 8 centimetres!!

Post-surgery, he seemed to cope really well for a few days, then went downhill fast, his bowel had packed up and as a consequence he had a heart attack and a couple of mini strokes. (Never underestimate the value of your butt hole, it is vital to life!!) He spent the next 5 weeks in intensive care, 3 weeks in high dependency, followed by another 3 months in various wards, learning how to walk again, he was as weak as a kitten. My big, healthy dad had shrunk to a little old frightened man, it was heart breaking!! He spent the next two years deteriorating slowly at home with us, tottering around on a walker, getting more and more frail. One afternoon, I was trying to get a nap on the sofa, when I heard a loud thump, then a shout, dad had fallen and broken his hip! This disaster resulted in him spending the next 4 weeks in hospital, his resources getting lower and lower, he eventually slipped away 6th November 2010 after watching Simon Cowell crucify some poor singer on The X Factor on TV, I always blamed Cowell!!

Whilst dad was alive, and during that last couple of years, I set him up with a doorbell all his very own, so that he could call me whenever he needed me night or day.

Towards the last few weeks, he was getting more and more frail and in need of more and more care, I had to give up the part-time job I had, as I kept falling asleep at my desk by 11am!! I was also dealing with a severely disabled, very aggressive daughter, not recommended if you need your sleep!! He got bed sores on his heels which he said stung like beestings, and bless him, he would ring that flaming bell up to 7 or 8 times a night! Needless to say, I was getting pretty tired by now!

After he passed, probably about a week, he started ringing that damn bell again – yes, I did say that, several times a night the bloody thing would ring, even after I threw it out!! Hubby would insist there must be someone at the front door, what 3am??? Having checked several times and assured him there was nobody at our front door, he eventually came to the same conclusion as me, dad was still very much around and wanted us to know that!!

The bell ringing carried on for about 5 or 6 weeks then tailed off, thank goodness, I did start to think he would carry on and on! I even went into his old room and 'had a word' about it, which did seem to do the trick!

To this day, some 7 years later, my severely disabled daughter still comes into me sometimes and says 'Gaddan' (her word for grandad), and 'goats', (her word for ghost). It's getting less and less as time goes on, if I think about it, she hasn't say either for quite a few months now, so perhaps he doesn't visit so often, or as she is now 18, she isn't quite so 'open' to him any more…who knows?? It was all very interesting at the time though.

***

When my dad was much younger, before he even got married, he and his brothers loved nothing more than going into town on a Saturday night and creating mayhem. When I say that, they used to get into fights, but, when they knocked someone to the floor, they would stop the fight and offer the loser a hand up and buy him a pint for his trouble. They were gentlemen lunatics!!

After one particular night, my dad related that he was walking home, this time alone, the other brothers were still in town, my dad had to be up early so was heading home and walking the 7 miles so that he could sober up on the way. He was fresh out of the army so thought nothing of a 7-mile march, he was striding along, head down, not thinking of anything in particular, when a very young policeman on a bike appeared at his side. Dad was about to say, 'good morning' when the copper started being rather brusque and aggressive towards him, demanding where he had been and where he was going, why was he walking down this road. Dad tried several times to explain, calmly to this snotty kid that he was walking home after a night out when that stupid idiot copper shoved dad and made him fall over. Well, that was the end of any pretence, he got what he deserved, royally, a good thump which knocked the idiot out, his bike was duly thrown over the hedge and dad continued on his way, albeit the other side of the hedgerows now and rather more quickly than he had planned.

It was all over the local papers the following Friday, police were hunting for 3 men apparently, who beat up this poor defenceless copper, he was going about his duty, only to be beaten up, his bike, he says, was stolen too!!

Well, my dad wasn't about to go to the police station to put them right, but he did laugh about it for years to come. They never did find those '3 vicious brutes!'

Another story he related to me some years ago was during the War, which dad was just too young to have to fight in, he was 15 when the War ended so did work on the farms and 'do his bit'. It was the night that Coventry was decimated, November 1940, dad was 10 at the time, he and a few mates were sat on a 5-bar gate watching the planes fighting and dropping bombs, they could clearly see the fires burning brightly in Coventry. They watched as one German plane headed towards where they were sat, it was very dark so there weren't worried about being seen. They watched as this plane headed off towards the village and to their surprise it dropped a bomb, they watched the bomb fall, in fact, they could actually hear it to, it whistled as it dropped. They waited for the explosion, but none came. They leaped down off the gate and headed to where they thought this bomb had landed, only to find nothing very much. It was too dark to have a really good look, so they went home and decided to meet up in the morning to investigate further.

The following morning, they went to the area they saw the bomb dropping towards and began a search. They found nothing, but an indentation in the mud behind the cricket pavilion. It had been very rainy in the past few weeks and there was a lot of mud. They came to the conclusion that the bomb must have been swallowed up by the mud, they rather foolishly tried poking the indentation with sticks, but found nothing. After another very thorough search of the entire area, they all agreed that their original thoughts were correct, the bomb had been swallowed up by the mud and was sat somewhere just behind the Cricket pavilion. They went off to tell someone, as clearly, it couldn't just be left.

The daftest thing… nobody believed them, the local councillors and village elders all decided they must have been mistaken, what did a bunch of 10-year olds know, and did absolutely nothing! When my dad died back in

2010, I decided that, as that field behind the cricket pavilion might one day be built upon, that someone in authority should actually be aware that there may still be a potentially dangerous UXB still sitting there waiting to be found. I phoned the local police who seemed to take the matter seriously, that is until the daft bugger went to the area I related, just as dad described and told me over the phone....'there's nothing to indicate that there is anything underground here'... I tried pointing out, that 'no', there wouldn't be any recent sign, (I omitted 'you daft bugger'), this all happened 14th November 1940... there wouldn't be any sign now!! That field had been plowed, planted, had cows on it, been used for village fete's etc, etc, there would not be any markings to indicate anything now!! Is it just me??

Well, I did my bit, so if you ever hear of a bomb going off behind a cricket pavilion in a small village in the midlands, don't say I didn't warn you!

# The Journey Home

I will write this in the form of a story. This really happened to someone I know, and they told me their story some years ago. Note: This was well before mobile phones were around! It all took place in and around the idyllic villages where I grew up. Names have been changed.

***

*Sarah was working late again, it was the third time this week and it was becoming a pain in the arse! It was late November, already really dark and raining cats and dogs! She really wasn't looking forward to the dash to the car, which was parked several streets away to avoid extortionate parking fees. She was just about to leave her desk when her mom phoned and asked her to pick up some milk on the way home, 'Typical' she thought, 'I just want to get straight home'... 'never mind, at least I will have some milk for a cup of tea' she thought to herself as she pulled on her raincoat and headed for the escalator and the exit.*

*She ran all the way to the car and arrived out of breath, jumped in and was never more thankful when the car started, it had taken three goes, and she had begun to panic! She cancelled her RAC membership a couple of months ago and really didn't want to break down anytime soon!*

*She headed off homeward, the journey normally took about 30 minutes, but that was in good weather, it was lashing down right now and the visibility was lousy! Sarah was straining her eyes to see the road ahead, which was very difficult as her route home was mainly country lanes, which didn't have any street lighting at all. She was about half way home, in an especially dimly lit area, trees both sides of the road and felt the car cough, she cursed under her breath, 'c'mon you little bugger, you can do it'. The car spluttered again, coughed loudly and the engine died, 'Damn and blast' she shouted, as she turned the wheel and coasted to a stop in the side of the road. It was still howling down and she was well and truly stranded! This was normally a very quiet road without the rain, so she didn't expect to see anyone else any time soon. Sarah sat in the car for about 20 minutes, hoping the rain would at least slow down a bit, it didn't, and the road was becoming a river! She was looking about, wondering what the heck to do next, when she noticed a cars' headlights approaching from behind. She had turned on her hazard lights, so wasn't worried about it running into her, heck, it was more likely to float past!!*

*She was feeling a little worried and wary when the car pulled up behind her, she couldn't see what type of car it was or who was driving it, it was so dark, and the headlights were so bright. She waited with not a small amount of trepidation, to see who would get out of the car. The drivers' door opened, and she saw someone getting slowly out, she still couldn't see who it was, they came towards her side of the car and she slowly cracked the window, just a little, just in case!! It was an old gentleman, he was vaguely familiar under his wet weather clothing, it was difficult to tell, she knew him from somewhere, just couldn't place him exactly. He leaned in close and asked, 'Do you need some help?' 'I've broken down' she replied hesitantly. 'I know nowt about cars, come and jump in mine and I'll drive you home, you're Dick Bentleys daughter, aren't you? he asked. She immediately felt better, it was someone her dad had*

*known, he sadly had died the previous year, she didn't*

*know if this chap actually knew.*

*She jumped out of her car and followed the old man back*

*to his car, jumping into the warmth was a relief. When*

*they were both sitting in the car, and ready for the off, he*

*turned to her and said, 'I was sorry to hear about your*

*dad, he was a smashing chap, missed by everyone I should*

*think?' 'Yes, he was, I miss him every day' Sarah said,*

*'Mom will be worried, I've been sat here for nearly half an*

*hour.' 'Don't worry love, I'll have you home in ten*

*minutes flat or my names not Bill Britton'! 'Bill Britton',*

*she thought to herself, 'that's his name, I remember him*

*now from when Dad was alive.' She felt much better now*

*and settled in for the drive home, true to his word it did*

*take only 10 minutes, they had a lovely chat on the way*

*too. She was however, very relieved to get into her home*

*and see her mom. Her mother was just getting to the stage of ringing the police...she was prone to overreact just a little! She was also pretty annoyed that Sarah hadn't picked up the milk! 'Typical' thought Sarah, 'I'm stranded, drenched, and finally saved by a good Samaritan, and all she can think about is the bloody milk'!!*

*'Where the hell have you been till this time?' 'Where's your car and who brought you home?' She was full of questions. Sarah didn't feel like answering them all right now and said so rather forcefully! 'I am not standing here explaining myself whilst I am cold, wet and miserable, I'm going for a shower!'*

*By the time she had showered and simmered down somewhat, she went back downstairs, and her mother was full of apologies. 'I'm really sorry I shouted at you, I was just so worried about you' her mom was truly full of remorse. Sarah couldn't stay angry with her for long and they soon began chatting amicably. 'So, what happened then love' said her mom, 'I broke down in the back lane, an old friend of Dad's came to my rescue.' 'Oh, who was that then?' She asked.*

*'It was old Bill Britton, he was lovely, brought me all the way home,' her mother stopped dead in her tracks, then shook her head in thought, said almost to herself. 'Can't be, maybe I'm mistaken, yes, that's it, I must have got it wrong.' Sarah listened with interest, 'what are you muttering about mother?' she asked. 'Well, it was just something I heard that's all, I must have got it wrong'. 'What did you hear?' Sarah asked, all interested now, it might be something juicy! 'Well, I thought I heard that Bill had died a few weeks ago, you know how the*

grapevine goes in these villages, I'm guessing the person who told me must have got it wrong, that's all'. 'Who told you that? He was very much alive a couple of hours ago, he drove me home, was lovely about Dad too!' Sarah was bemused and then amused when her mother told her it was Val at the post office who told her. 'Val, at the post office? She spreads more gossip than Woman's Own' Sarah laughed out loud. So, did her mother, she must have gotten that one completely wrong, and was going to be 'put straight' the next day, that was for sure!!

They had their evening meal and went off to bed, glad to be snug and warm and full of food whilst that damn storm kept on raging outside, rattling the windows and bending the trees.

The next morning, there was a break in the weather and the sun came out, bright and shiny, everything looked new and clean and fresh. Sarah was delighted with the *sunshine and went up to the local garage on foot to ask them to tow in her car and get it repaired. After she had done that, she went back home and got her bicycle out of the shed, checking the tyres and brakes, all seemed fine, she mounted up and decided to head to the next village to personally thank Bill for his help last night.*

*Her poor old legs were like jelly by the time she had cycled the 3 miles to the next village, she went up the main road, trying to locate the house where Bill and his wife lived, she spotted his old Morris Minor in the drive and went up to the front door and knocked.*

*Emily, Bills' wife answered the knock after a short while and Sarah was pleased to see that she hadn't changed much from the last time she had seen her about 5 years ago. Emily stood there, a quizzical look on her face at first, then she recognised Sarah and asked her in. 'I can't stop long' Sarah followed her into the lounge. She looked around expectantly, hoping to see Bill.*

*'I was so sorry to hear about your lovely Dad' Emily looked sadly at Sarah as she said this. Sarah was just about getting used to people coming out with it now and could answer without feeling like she wanted to cry.*

*'Thank you, Emily, I can't believe he's been gone nearly a year, we all miss him so much', Sarah actually felt close to tears, despite thinking she could talk about it now, there was something in Emily demeanour that brought all the sadness out!*

*'What can I do for you Sarah?' Emily finally asked after making a cup of tea and offering a large slab of cake!*

*'Well, I was hoping to see Bill, so I could thank him for saving me last night' Sarah said, 'he literally saved my life!' Emily gasped, seemed taken aback and went very*

pale and quiet. 'What's wrong Emily, what did I say?' She was seriously worried about Emily keeling over, she had gone really pale, it was a few moments before Emily could form a sentence.

'What did you say? Why would you say that, it's not true, it's just too cruel, is this some sort of sick joke?'


Sarah was aghast, 'No, what, wait, what do you mean a sick joke? He was lovely and helped me out, took me right home in all that rain, couldn't thank him enough, that's why I am here, my car broke down and he helped me' Sarah was gabbling now, as Emily was openly crying and gasping for breath, she sat down with a thump in her chair and took a large sip of tea. 'Are you seriously telling me that my Bill helped you out, last night you say?' 'Yes, he stopped in the rain after I broke down, he picked me up *and drove me home, we had a lovely chat and I just wanted to say a big thank you to him for that' said Sarah.*

*Emily just sat there, looking Sarah in the eye as if weighing up what she had just said. 'And he picked you up in his Morris Minor?' questioned Emily, who was a little shaky and still pale. Sarah was quite concerned for her. 'Where is Bill, shall I fetch him, if you are feeling ill?' Sarah offered. With that, Emily's' damn finally burst and she began openly crying, this was a disaster thought Sarah, what the hell was wrong with this woman?*

*Emily finally pulled herself together enough to splutter out the words 'He died', then she started crying again. 'I know, I do miss my dad too.' Said Sarah. 'No, not your dad, my Bill, my Bill died 4 weeks ago.' Emily blurted out. Sarah froze, then remembered her conversation with her mother last night. She couldn't process this information and sat there with her mouth opening and closing with nothing coming out. Emily took pity on her and said, more kindly this time, 'he died of a heart attack, here in this front room about a month ago'.*

*Sarah was dumfounded, literally and couldn't form a sentence in her head. 'What the hell?? What did this mean? This just can't be, it just can't' she thought to herself. Emily then stood up and gestured for Sarah to follow her, they went back out into the front garden where the car was parked. 'You say he picked you up in this car?' She asked. Sarah looked at the car and said 'Yes, it was raining so badly, it was lovely and warm, and he took me home, but.... how can that be?' She said almost to herself. Emily then pointed to the drive behind the car, which was parked facing the house, 'look at the grass' she said. Sarah looked and was dumfounded to see that the grass had grown high, was not crushed down in any way shape or form. This car had NOT moved in weeks!! Sarah felt her legs buckle under her, Emily grabbed her arm and walked her back into the house. 'This can't be happening' thought Sarah. 'What the hell happened to me?'*

*Emily sat Sarah down and poured her another cup of tea, a good strong one this time, and Sarah was grateful for that. She looked round the room and saw photos of Bill with Emily and their family in better days, his smile was still the same as the one he gave her last night…'What the hell am I thinking?' 'He cannot have smiled at me last night as he was DEAD last night'. Sarah went all cold and started shaking.*

*Emily was talking to her again. 'Tell me what actually happened, are you absolutely certain it was my Bill?'*

*Sarah nodded towards one of the photos and confirmed that yes, it was definitely Bill, there was no doubt in her mind at all. Emily began to quietly weep, Sarah felt like joining in, this was not a situation that you ever expected to come across!*

*They sat there for the next couple of hours trying to find an explanation for what Sarah had experienced, obviously this was not easy to explain away and Emily offered to phone Sarah's mom to come and fetch her. Sarah turned her down, she still had her cycle and needed the time it was going to take getting home to try and sort out her thoughts. She went out to get her cycle, looked again at that car and saw a spider had made numerous webs inside of the car, it had a cracked window and looked completely abandoned.*

*Sarah cycled home and sat down with her mother to try and work out what the hell had happened, between them, they concluded that Bill was just being Bill, helping a friend out who was in desperate need, that was just how he was.*

# The Old Devon Cob House

This was a lovely old Devon Cob house owned by someone I used to know, whom I will call Richard, who lived in it whilst renovating. It was massive, it had once been 2 cottages and, now it was being renovated as a single house once again.

Whilst the renovations were going on, the owner noticed that several odd things were happening, the main one being late at night with the bedroom door opening and shutting loudly, followed by footsteps all the way down the hall. It was pretty unnerving if you weren't expecting it. A stray cat had taken up residence in the house too, which was not unwelcome, there was a bit of a mouse problem. This cat would always sleep in that bedroom and on the bed with whomever was sleeping there, never seemed bothered by the 'invisible' visitor, indeed, would seem to watch something/someone invisible crossing the room!

The bathroom seemed to be the main focus of attention there, with various people feeling 'watched' whilst they were showering, and not being able to use anything electrical like toothbrushes or electric razors in that room. These items would work perfectly normally outside the room, but once you entered, they would stubbornly refuse to work!

Having stayed there frequently with my kids, I could attest to the reputation of the place. I loved the old spiral staircase in the corner of the main lounge, it was accessed through an old oak latched door, it was said to have been made of old ships timbers and had been in place for at least a couple of hundred years, so the age of those ships timbers must have been extreme! I was never bothered by anything truly spooky until the very last time I stayed there. That was when, in the early hours, I could clearly hear footsteps going along the hall, I leapt up and looked out quietly, and although the footsteps could still be clearly heard, there was simply nobody there! My dad also stayed there a few times and he says that he was woken several times by the 'night stalker'. A few of the villagers also stated that they had seen someone looking out of the windows when the place was empty. Even to the extent that the police were called once, they gained entry (which was not difficult as the person who owned the place never bothered to lock it unless he was going on holiday!) searched the house and found nothing untoward.

# The Pub

Having worked in a number and pubs over the years, and drank in a great many more! I can say that most, although 'atmospheric', were probably not haunted. The one that does stick in my mind though wasn't your typical pub, it was in fact, a converted sports shop on the High Street. It was a narrow, tall building with four floors, five if you counted the attic.

The first floor housed an old range with a bread oven, it hadn't been used in many years, but just occasionally the landlady would report walking into that room and getting the impression of a stout lady standing in front of the range, as if stirring a pot. The landlady reported that the first time this happened, she swore the lady turned towards her when she let out a startled screech, then faded slowly away!

The bar area, although not massive was also 'atmospheric' and I can attest to hearing a disembodied 'sneeze/cough' when I was in the building entirely alone one morning, I had been cleaning and stocking shelves ready for the mornings business, I never did find a reasonable explanation for that damn 'sneeze'!

The locals themselves could be pretty hair raising in the normal order of things, I particularly remember one lunchtime, we had been reasonably quiet, when all of a sudden, a group of local lads came into the pub, there was probably 7 or 8 of them, I had been dealing with some money and had my back turned when they came into the bar. When I turned around they were all stood at the bar, wearing identical 'T' shirts and stupid grins, everyone else in the pub had seen what I obviously hadn't!! I started to pour them drinks, when as one, they all backed 3 steps from the bar so that I could see them from the waist down, they then, at a signal from their 'leader' yanked up their shirts revealing the, by now obvious truth, that they wore nothing else......the sight of those daft buggers still makes me laugh to this day, they were all stark bollock naked from the waist down, one of the lads has been known as 'Whon Hung Lo' ever since, for obvious reasons!!

What I hadn't spotted was that the lad I had been working with had 'done a runner', I couldn't work out where he had gone, until a few minutes later he returned, out of breath, chuckling like the idiot he was. 'Where the heck have you been, you should have seen those daft buggers' I said laughingly to him. He just laughed loud and long, and told me that as soon as he spotted what they were up to he had ran to the pub next door, where they had hailed from, and hidden all their clothes!!

Another day saw another drunken idiot wanting to fight everyone, he was known as a wife beater, used to back her into a corner and when he thought nobody was looking, would thump her in the face, lovely chap!! (Not!) This particular occasion he was being even more of an idiot than usual, shouting how he was going to hit everyone, ranting and swearing. His one liner was classic, if not boring in the extreme….'You're dead, you're dead and you're dead', accompanied by jabbing his pudgy finger at everyone in the pub!! 'Yeah, yeah, whatever', I thought!

It was a quiet lunch hour and I was behind the bar. There were 3 or 4 locals in the bar and another couple sitting quietly on one of the tables, trying to have a quiet conversation and ignore that bloody idiot. The locals were trying to persuade him to leave quietly, they had been doing this for some 10 or 15 minutes and were getting absolutely nowhere, he was just getting louder and more obnoxious!! I was getting pretty fed up with the situation and wanted him out, before we lost the nice young couple in the bar. Eventually I just said loudly 'For Gods' sake, will someone just hit the bugger?'

With that, the young man, sat with his young lady, stood up, placed his pint on the bar in front of me, saying 'watch my beer' and walked over towards the idiot, with all the locals surrounding him trying to placate him, said gently, 'excuse me ladies' when they parted, he pulled back a fist and knocked the bugger flat out on the floor. Funniest thing I think I have ever seen!! The local lads lifted his dazed, bruised form off the floor and before he could do anything about it, they took him outside and laid him very gently on the pavement. My hero meanwhile, calmly walked back to the bar, where I had pulled him a fresh pint 'on the house,' collected his drink and went back to his quiet conversation with his girlfriend. Never have I seen a more deserving wife beater get some of his own medicine. It was pure gold!!

# Dizzy Heights

This was a flat I lived in with my husband when we first got married, it was a second floor flat, entered by a long flight of stairs, hence the name!! (That and the fact that we spent an awful lot more time in the pub in those days than was strictly necessary). We used to kid ourselves we weren't going out for more than 'one' drink, would put a couple of jacket potatoes in the oven, get back 4 hours later to two small charcoal hot smoking lumps!!

After I have been living there with hubby for about a month, I remember that very early one morning I was lying awake, just drifting in and out of a lovely snooze. I had been up and made a cup of tea and was just enjoying that, and listening to hubby snoring loudly, rattling the windows. I remember distinctly the door slowly opening and an elderly lady in light blue pyjamas enter the room, carrying a cup of tea, one of those old-fashioned cups and saucers, she had her head down, no doubt concentrating on not spilling her tea. She didn't look in my direction, or appear conscious of my presence at all. I watched her walk slowly round the end of the bed and disappear before my eyes! I lay there, totally gobsmacked, couldn't quite believe what I had seen. Had I actually just seen that? Was it a dream? I just couldn't work it out. You can bet I was wide awake now. I didn't bother to wake 'his knibbs' as I actually didn't think he would believe me, probably think it was down to a hangover or something similar!

That very same thing happened to me twice in that flat, she was all bent up, had long ratty white hair, very thin and aged and her pyjamas were probably two sizes too big. The second time, I was actually much more startled than the first, I guess that was probably because it actually confirmed that I wasn't dreaming the first time, and that this was actually real! She followed exactly the same path and disappeared just as before, very odd!

That flat had another nasty scare in store for me, the bedroom was quite small, and the wardrobe was right next to the bed. One early evening, after the events above, I was having an early night, had just gotten into bed and was reading my book, just settling myself down to sleep. Out of the corner of my eye I could see movement, very slow movement. The wardrobe doors were opening, very slowly. I lay there watching in both horror and fascination, wondering what the heck was going to happen next, the entire contents of the wardrobe very slowly fell across the bed in a massive heavy pile. I nearly died of shock, and no, it wasn't paranormal, it was the poor old wardrobe being asked to cope with twice the contents it was actually designed for and giving up on the struggle in spectacular style. I laughed afterwards, but at the time, I really thought the hounds of hell were going to come out of that damn wardrobe!

# The Bungalow

This was a white bungalow we lived in a few years ago, I won't name it or the street, as there is a family living there now, and as I have said previously in this book, if they haven't seen or heard anything, I really don't want them to either go looking, or feel frightened, as there is really nothing to be frightened of in this this place.

We lived there for about 10 years, never felt anything, all very nice, quiet, normal house. Until one Christmas I bought my son one of those ATM cash machines you could get for your kids a few years back. I thought it would help him save some money and he would enjoy using the keys, calculator etc. All the number keys made a separate noise, just like you get on real ATM's, it turned itself off after 10 minutes of being idle, was really cute to look at and my son loved it.

A few days after we had the machine, it was left downstairs, switched off. About 2 or 3 am I heard some strange noises coming from downstairs, our bedroom was directly above the lounge. I lay there listening for a while, trying to work out what it was, I must have drifted back off to sleep as the next time I became conscious the alarm was going off! I thought no more about it and went on with my day.

That night, again about 3am, I heard some noises again downstairs, I sat up in bed listening intently. I realised then that it was my son's toy ATM – the key sounds were going off! Strange, I thought, that thing should be turned off, I got up and went downstairs to investigate, it was turned on and hadn't switched itself off suggesting that it had been used in the last 20 minutes! I went back upstairs, and lay down, before I had a chance to go to sleep, the bloody thing started again. This time I woke up hubby as I really wanted to know that I wasn't going completely bonkers!

Yes, he could hear it to, he said it was 'nothing' which basically means, it's 'something' but I am not going to be the one to find out what!!

I lay there for half an hour listening and there were odd tonal noises that were clearly the keys of that damn ATM going off. I decided it must have a glitch, or a bug crawling round inside the works, shorting the terminal and making it go off. I determined that the next morning I would have the thing apart and take a look for myself!

The next day, I was there with my screwdriver, the list of instructions, and a determination to find out what was going on once and for all. The thing NEVER went off in the daytime when the kids were at school, so there didn't seem to be a delay timer on it. It was bug free and I could find nothing wrong with the wiring, all wires were correctly attached and to the appropriate places. I tried to press the buttons whilst it was turned off, to see if it would go off, it didn't. This was a bit of a mystery!

I left it downstairs again that night, and again, the bloody thing was going off again, I shot downstairs to see who/what was doing it, all was quiet, however, it was turned on once again! I had had enough by now and brought the thing up to our bedroom, switched it off and stuck it on the dressing table, watching it like a hawk.

That bloody thing <u>never</u> went off whilst in our bedroom or indeed anywhere upstairs, it was, after a lengthy process of elimination, ONLY when it was left in the lounge, work that one out???
I never did work out what was happening in that house, could find no explanation whatsoever. Another oddity!

# The Car Crash

One winters evening, myself and two others were in the car with my mother, going to some antique preview in a distant town, I cannot recall too much more about that particular side of events.

On the journey out, we had to cross a crossroads in the middle of nowhere. There were lights in the distance as we approached, you could see a police car flashing away, and, as we go closer, there was a car in the tree, yes, in the bloody tree, it was right up the tree! There was another car in the ditch on the other side of the road, on its' roof and the police were trying to sort it all out and get ambulances on scene.

We carried on our journey, chatting about the accident and wondering how in the hell that car got up the bloody tree, it must have been going at one hell of a speed! We arrived for our preview meeting, and unfortunately, it had been cancelled, so we had to turn around and head back home.

It was about 5 miles back out to the crash site, and as we approached from the distance, we could see 2 ambulances had also joined the scene and it was a mass of flashing lights. It didn't look good, we were discussing whether to stop and offer assistance, as my mom was a trained nurse, when on the side of the road we could see someone standing, looking towards the crash. This was about 200 yards from the actual accident, well out of range of any lights, in fact the figure was in total darkness and only lit up by the headlights of our car.

Now, I find this hard to believe, and I saw the bloody thing, but it was hugely tall figure, probably 7ft, in a dark or black habit type outfit, with a hood over its' head. I got the impression that it was also very thin. It was just standing there, facing towards the crash site, with the hood flapping gently in the breeze. As we passed it, I remember saying quite loudly and in a startled voice, 'did you see that?' to which my mother (if you've read this book so far, you will know by now she could shout LOUD!), screeched, 'DON'T LOOK BACK'. Well, after that, the hounds of hell wouldn't let my neck stretch to look back at that figure. There was nothing on the side of the road on the way out, so it wasn't something daft like a road sign with a bin liner wrapped around it, in fact, I don't even think bin liners were invented back then. All the fields around were 'prairie farmed' which meant that most of the hedges were ripped out in order to make more profit out of the land, so you could see for quite a distance.

We all saw it, none of us knew what it could be, but we spent the entire journey home speculating. Still to this day, I wonder what that was, three of us are still alive from that day and all can remember it clearly. It makes me cringe ever so slightly just thinking about it even after all these years! What it could have been, I have no idea, and I am so glad we didn't stop to find out either.

As a postscript there were 2 deaths at that roadside crash all those years ago, very sad.

# 1973, That Terrible Year

My brother, Freddy, was just 16 when he got killed in a terrible accident at the end of the lane where we lived. He had left at 8.30am for work on his bicycle and was racing, trying to catch up with his mates who were a few hundred yards ahead. He could see them from the lane, they had already crossed the main A444 and could be seen in the

distance heading towards their place of work just outside of Twycross village. Freddy had only been there 3 weeks, and presumably didn't want to turn up after his friends. He hurtled down the lane and, as described by the driver of the car, and his friends who had stopped to let him catch up. He rode straight out into the path of an oncoming car and was terribly injured, he died an hour later from his injuries. About two weeks before this happened, he had spent a Sunday afternoon sat in the kitchen with my mom, just chatting away. He started talking about what he wanted to happen if he died, how he would like his funeral arranged, what he wanted everyone to wear, what songs he would like etc., my mother was a bit freaked out, and told him to stop being so bloody morbid. He was a fit, healthy 16-year-old, had just left school, started a new job and gotten his first girlfriend and here he was organising his bloody funeral? She shushed him up and told him not to be so daft, nothing like that was going to happen for years. Little did she know??

As it happened, we would be arranging his funeral before the month was out. At least we knew what he would have wanted, how he didn't want anyone wearing black, what songs he wanted….it was all so bloody sad!

That year, 1973, was the worst in living history (apart from the War), for deaths locally. My brother was the first in May, two weeks later his best friend from school also got killed in a road accident, he lived in the next village. Shortly after that there began a series of 6 further deaths in the surrounding villages over the coming months. The year was not done yet, and in the October of that year, we also lost my lovely Aunt who fell off the back of a potato wagon being towed by a tractor and died. We were all wondering by now, would it never end?

Another local chap, a friend of both of my brothers came to our house and sat down with my mom for a chat. She would never forget what he said that day in November 1973. He told my mom that she shouldn't feel so bad about Freddy dying, as, he had been so badly injured, that if he had lived, he would have been a 'cabbage in a wheelchair' for the rest of his life and nobody would want that!

Christmas Eve saw that lovely chap out with his girlfriend and another couple in a car, they hit a patch of ice and shot off the road. The only person injured was that same lad, he was so severely injured he spent the rest of his life 'a cabbage in a wheelchair'. You couldn't make it up, could you?

That horrible year was whispered about in hushed tones for many years to come, it was almost as if the Devil himself had come to visit our little communities. So many lives destroyed, kids left without a mother, sisters without brothers and families torn apart. I hope never to see the like again!

# The 'Crisis' Apparition

My aunt Cynthia was a lovely woman, the 'salt of the Earth' type person that everyone couldn't help but warm to. She had been ill for a while and required hospitalisation for a rupture repair in her abdomen. She had worked for years on a nursery smallholding and thought nothing of throwing sacks of potatoes and soil around. Unfortunately, her body thought otherwise, when the surgeon opened her abdomen to do the repair, he found that her lower abdomen was literally 'full of holes, like an Emmental Cheese' were his actual words!

The half hour operation turned into a four-hour job, with various complications. Nevertheless, she seemed to be getting over it well, to such an extent that she was being discharged within a few days of the operation, the surgical team were very pleased with her progress as they felt she was a very fit person for her age. I guess lumping all that stuff round the nursery would keep you pretty fit!

Her mom was a lovely old lady, she was delighted that Cynthia was due home and planned to bake a lovely cake to welcome her. The hospital discharge was set for Monday afternoon, and preparations were afoot to make sure everything was ready for the 'invalid'. Cynthia's mom began baking her cake mid-morning, she had plenty of time and planned to decorate it before heading off to welcome her daughter home.

She had just gotten the cake out of the oven and was 'prodding' it with a knitting needle to see if it was ready, when suddenly she felt all the hair on her body stand on end. She couldn't understand why, until she looked up and saw Cynthia standing in the kitchen. She couldn't quite believe what she was seeing, and initially thought Cynthia had been released early. She spoke to her, asked her what she was doing home early, explained she was baking a cake and would have to rush it now. When she finished her sentence, she looked more closely at Cynthia, she was just stood there, not moving, not speaking, just standing, looking sad. Her mom relayed that she then realised that this was not 'normal', the 'apparition' wasn't 'solid' and seemed to have fuzzy edges. As she came to realise what this might mean, the apparition simply faded away and was gone.

Her mom knew without a doubt what that meant, and she sat down to await the call that she knew would inevitably come. It took 45 minutes, but the call came, Cynthia had died quite suddenly and unexpectedly at the hospital. It was later found that she had had a blood clot break off and travel to her lungs which caused her sudden death.

This type of apparition is called a 'crisis apparition' and is more common than you would think. When my mom died, I wrote earlier in this book that I was convinced that someone came rushing into the room and sat down next to me on the sofa. Unlike Cynthia's mom, I couldn't see anything, but that didn't stop it being a very real, and very surreal experience. There was **definitely** someone in that room with me, I just didn't know at the time what it all meant, it was only a few days later, when I had time to sit down and evaluate all that had happened, that I realised it must have been my mother. The phone had rung within a couple of minutes of this occurrence happening, and, as my mother died instantly it would mean that the very moment of her death is when I had that experience. Too much of a coincidence for me!

# Hotel Ghosts & Guests!

I have worked in a couple of hotels and known a few people who have worked in a great many more.

I used to work with a chef, Dave, who had a rather startling story to tell of a hotel he worked in many years ago. The hotel was based in Taunton and he was a commis chef, which basically means the lowest of the low, the person who did all the food prepping, cleaning up afterwards and was in line for being shouted at if anything went wrong.

He was nearly always there on his own most afternoons, prepping all the vegetables, supervising meat roasting, washing salads, in fact anything and everything. He was also called upon to bake the cakes that were served up mid-afternoon, as let's face it, three full meals a day is not nearly enough to eat, you ALWAYS need tea and cakes at 4pm just to see you through to dinner at 7pm, that is rather a long stretch to go without filling your face!!

He was beavering away and was all alone as usual. The door at the far end of the kitchen opened and a young boy entered the kitchen, he was, as Dave described, wearing shorts and a sleeveless jumper, with a button-down check shirt underneath. Dave thought he was a normal kid, one of the guests who had wandered off. He watched the boy and fully intended to ask the lad where he was going. As the boy approached, he broke into a run, Dave was cutting carrots up and watched, fascinated to see where he was heading to. He ran straight past Dave, went around the end of the stainless-steel work station and ran straight through a wall!!

Dave said he just stood there, knife in hand, he didn't fully understand what he had just witnessed, he had actually started to speak to the child as he ran past and hadn't quite gotten his sentence out when that darn kid did the disappearing act through the wall. What was most perplexing is that this kid looked totally normal in every way.

Dave stated to me a few years after this event that he could still see this kid in his mind's eye. After the event, he realised that the boy was actually wearing clothes more befitting a child of the 1950's. After he got over the initial shock, he mentioned this apparition to some of the other staff he worked with and it turned out that this child was seen quite regularly and had died of choking in the restaurant some years earlier and was indeed a child of the 1950's, his parents being previous owners of the hotel.

Another story that came down to me over the period I worked in the hotel trade was related by one of the staff who boarded in the attic rooms at the top of the hotel. She was a waitress and regularly kept late hours. Many times, when she headed off to bed, absolutely knackered from the late evening dinners we sometimes did, she would flop down on the sofa in her rooms and watch TV for an hour or two before going to bed as she was just too wired from the running around to contemplate sleep.

She would be sitting there watching her TV and stated that many times she would see shadowy figures moving around under the door to the corridor outside her rooms. She would see quite clearly dark shadows moving as if someone was moving around in the hall. She would never hear anything, and when it first happened she actually got up and went to her door, opening it onto the upper corridor, only to find it completely empty! After that, she just let it happen and decided to leave it well and truly alone, and I don't blame her, I would not have liked living up there even without the shadows!

Working in hotels brings about its' own entertainment and we had plenty of incidents of a humorous nature to keep us chuckling! One Christmas in particular was hilarious, if you had a strong stomach that is!! There was a full house, mostly elderly, all eating and drinking like it was going out of fashion, three full 3 or 5 course meals a day, plus tea and cakes in the afternoon.  It only surprised me that it took 3 days before they started getting really ill from all that overindulgence!  Two little old ladies in particular, who were hilarious and mostly drunk, called me to help them in the lift one afternoon.  I duly trotted off to see what they wanted, and was repulsed to see that one of them had been sick in the corner of the lift, not only that, she had lost her false teeth in that loathsome pile and she wanted ME to fish the bloody things out.  This would require a strong stomach, rubber gloves and plenty of disinfectant.  I duly fished out the offending item and returned it to a very tipsy 80-year-old who was having trouble standing, she had partaken of the Port rather more than a little!

Another time, we were serving a 'late dinner' for the local Stroke Club…. you're way ahead of me now eh??  Yes, half way through the dinner, someone had a stroke, we were just clearing the main course when a poor gentleman slumped into his napkin.  An ambulance was duly called and to my utter astonishment, when the ambulance men were carting this poor sap out of the dining room over the heads of the other diners, they were shoving them aside to order sweet! It was as if nothing untoward had happened, there were literally people standing up, leaning over and pushing the stretcher aside in order to make sure we got the right sweet order! Hilarious!

We had our share of guests who never left too…by that I mean they checked out, literally! One lovely couple were firm favourites with us waitresses as they actually treated us like people instead of downtrodden slaves! One evening, during the Christmas madness, the husband died in the early hours, his wife had heard him struggling with his last breath and instead of calling anyone, or indeed an ambulance, she simply sat with his dead body until 8am when the staff came on duty, even then she didn't want a fuss, said not to call the funeral home before everyone had gone down for breakfast as she didn't want them upset by seeing his body being removed. What a lovely, thoughtful daft old lady that was! You know, she came back every couple of years and insisted in staying in that very same room!

Another time and elderly gentleman 'checked out' during breakfast, he was eating porridge and literally slumped over, his head in the porridge, we waitresses were horrified and in a total panic, not knowing quite what to do. A lady from a nearby table got up, went over to the elderly gentleman, felt for a pulse, stated to nobody in particular that he was dead and went back and ate a hearty breakfast!! We found out later that she was a retired Matron, which I suppose would go some way towards explaining her nonchalance to, what was to us, rather startling and unsettling! Another ambulance, another stretcher and this time, the guests were demanding coffee and toast like nothing out of the ordinary was happening!

During the summer months we always had a full house, usually a coach load from the Sunderland area, salt of the Earth people with such a lovely sense of humour, at least to me anyway! Many evenings we staff would head out clubbing and not get in until the wee small hours, usually hammered! We would then turn up for work by 7.30am and attempt to look sober and serve breakfast to 90 very hungry northern folk. Many mornings we would take in it turns to run out to the back toilet to vomit, before returning pale faced to serve greasy bacon and eggs to the hoards! I can remember quite clearly one morning we had an order for boiled eggs, they were duly dropped in the pan and after a short while the chef called that they were ready. I duly delivered them to the lady who requested them and went to stand by my station waiting to see if anyone else wanted anything. I was watching this lady having a very in-depth chat with the other people on her table when she bashed the egg rather forcefully and we were both horrified when the damn thing splashed very uncooked egg white all over the table. The chef had given me the raw eggs instead of the cooked ones, I don't know who was more likely to vomit, me or her!! It took a lot of placating to get her back on side!

Another time, we had a massive thunderstorm and I was just heading out to the dining room with an armful of hot platefuls of food, when one of my ladies from the table nearest the kitchen passed me on the way out, I was a bit dumfounded, but had an armful of food to deliver to a nearby table, so just had to carry on. When I got back in the kitchen area, I found said lady hiding under the stairs whimpering like a whipped puppy, the reason? She didn't like thunder!!

That same week we also had a 'choker' and it was down to me to do the Heimlich manoeuvre in order to save the poor saps life! I duly got behind this large middle-aged bloke and it took a couple of 'pulls' before he deposited a large lump of cornflakes on the table. My thanks? None at all from that table, nothing whatsoever was said, in fact, at the end of the week, when it came time to leave our tips, that bloody table left 20p!! Oh, how we hated it when the new 20p coin came out, they really thought they were giving you something. I would invariably return it to them, with a big cheesy smile and say, 'you need it more than me love'!!! If you do it with a smile, you can get away with almost anything!!

That particular dining room did have one paranormal occurrence that had me thinking. It was before the season began, the dining room was empty, and I had been setting tables, cleaning and polishing all morning getting ready for that guests that were due in a couple of days. All was quiet, there was just myself and another girl, we were having a cup of tea, not saying anything, just enjoying the peace, when from behind the pillar where we were sat came an almighty sneeze. We both nearly spat out our tea and jumped up to see who was behind the pillar, we did a pincer movement and met the other side, there was nobody there! That was the only time we ever heard it, we never did work out who or what did it, another of life's mysteries!!

One Sunday morning, leading up to Christmas, the guests were yet to arrive and were due the following lunchtime. All of us staff were busy decorating, polishing, cooking, cleaning and generally making the place splendid for the guests. We had a break mid-morning and most of us were sat around a table in the dining room having a cup of tea and a late breakfast. The Chefs were in the kitchen dealing with the Turkeys which had been delivered a couple of hours previously. The dining room door swung open and in strutted both Chefs looking mightily pleased with themselves, they were rather bloodied and still in their aprons. We looked over, wondering what the stupid grins on their faces what about, when, at some unspoken signal they both whipped back their aprons to reveal, what look to us like two enormous penises, over a foot long each. We shrieked and laughed when we realised that, what looked, like massive willy's were in fact Turkey necks, which they had tucked into their trousers!! All this, of course, before Political Correctness told us what was funny and what was not!!

On another occasion, I thought I would get my own back on one of the Chefs who had been particularly bossy of late. There were some boiled eggs in a bowl on the side in the kitchen and I decided I would grab one and smash it on the Chef's forehead for a laugh!! Well, the laugh was on me, little did I know those eggs were in fact uncooked, he said the look on my face when I smashed that egg on his forehead was worth all the mess!

Another hotel I worked in way back in the day, we used to have an old people's home come to visit us every October for an afternoon meal, which was right at the end of the summer season. This was a regular thing, and looked forward to by all concerned. This particular 'old people's home' was more like and elderly 'St Trinians'. They would turn up and take it in turns getting into the lift to get down one floor to the dining room, there wasn't more than a couple that were capable of making it down the stairs. This was the first hurdle, and consequently where the arguments started. They would almost come to blows about who was getting in the lift with whom. There was one lady in a wheelchair who never let us down when she visited. She would be wheeled out of the lift and this took her past the bar area and on into the dining room. She would spot the bar like a sniffer dog, throw herself dramatically out of her wheelchair and onto the floor, where she would lie, whimpering alarmingly. The first time she did it, we were all deeply concerned, worried she was hurt, there was talk about whether to call an ambulance, doctor etc. She forestalled all this fuss by making a 'huge' effort to sit upright and demand 'Brandy', 'please, get me a Brandy' she whimpered. Of course, poor saps that we were, we complied immediately, she must be in shock, we worried that she may have broken a hip or worse…

That is, until the wiley old bugger did the same thing the next year, and every year thereafter until her eventual demise at the grand old age of 90! I understand she could spot a bar a mile off, and her carers actually threatened to strap her into her chair if she did it again. I just love old people like that!! I did forestall her one year, I think it was the last time I saw her, when she came out of the lift, heading towards the dreaded bar, I stood there with a Brandy in hand, and said something like, 'Save yourself the trouble, here's your Brandy'. I swear she was really pissed off with me for doing that, she had been done out of her 'moment' of fame!

The others in her group were only slightly less alcoholic, their interest lay more in the field of romance!! We used to get them all sat down and wait for the fun to begin. If we hadn't got them seated with their particular friend, there would be hell to pay. Two elderly ladies actually came to blows over the gentleman who was sat with them.

He seemed bemused; or was it 'amused' to see his 'girlfriends' getting down and dirty over his favours!  They were actually calling each other 'slags' and 'slappers', their being well in their 80's made it even more hilarious!!  They would call us over to the tables, demanding large sherry, Port, Brandy and anything else they could get their hands on.  Their carers would try to put a stop to it after one or two drinks, but by then it was getting riotous.  Rickety old hips would be swinging, trying to dance along to the background music we always played.  Zimmer frames clacking together,
ladies would be dancing with ladies as there were never enough men to go around.  They would inevitably overindulge both with food and booze, the resulting chaos always reminded me of a chimp's tea party at Twycross Zoo I used to love to watch when I was a child!!

By the time they were getting ready to leave, there would usually be blocked toilets where they had tried to flush the large pads many of them wore.  There would be copious amounts of food thrown around the room, it was never more fun than when they started a 'bun fight'.

Occasionally one or more would vomit, sometimes losing hearing aids, false teeth, glasses or anything else that could fall off into that vile pile!!

Every year we REALLY looked forward to the chaos, hilarity and downright fun those elderly people would visit upon us, they were fabulous!!  I sincerely hope they are still doing the same in the next life!

Printed in Great Britain
by Amazon

80836760R00089